Mirror, Mirror:
Reflections of the Sacred Self

Patricia Telesco

Mirror, Mirror: Reflections of the Sacred Self
A Blue Star Productions Publication

ISBN 1-881542-51-3
Copyright © 1999 by Patricia Telesco
Cover Design: Colleen Koziara
An Original Paperback

Published by Blue Star Productions
A Division of Book World, Inc.
9666 E Riggs Rd #194, Sun Lakes AZ 85248

First Printing: January 1999

Be sure to visit our web site at:
www.bkworld.com

Other Books by Patricia Telesco
Published by Blue Star Productions:

Through-the-Year Series:
365 Days of Prosperity
365 Days of Luck
365 Days of Health

Dedication

To the sense of resplendence
that comes from within
and the self assurance
to manifest it without

Table of Contents

Introduction

"Mirror, Mirror, on the wall
who's the fairest of them all?"
— The Evil Queen, *Snow White*

In a society strongly shaped by external perception, what we do for "appearance sake" becomes a query into our sense of priorities. It is also a definitive reflection of culture and mores as a whole. While the neo-revolutionary movements of the 1960's attempted to banish conventional ideas by releasing unrealistic expectations, today we find ourselves no less affected by the concept of comeliness. Amidst our modern, logical world, many people continue to believe that a pleasing physical framework is somehow essential to self-worth.

How often do you hear friends, family members, and total strangers alike remarking about the curve of a nose or a few extra pounds when they pass a mirror? While we sometimes interpret such comments as superficial, the *emotional* impact of self images is not a superficial matter at all. It is something that reaches far beyond that reflective surface, effecting the heart and soul of humankind.

A portion of human nature yearns to be what a civilization or culture dictates as being handsome or beautiful. No matter how *enlightened* we think we are, impressions about our personal appearance touches every corner of our life. When one suddenly discovers that they cannot fit the ideal mold, the crushing feeling of inadequacy can be overwhelming.

It's natural to seek some form of approval in the eyes of friends and family, that's part of the tribal mind from which humankind sprang. Yet, how can we begin to recognize that approval when no acceptance stares back at us from the proverbial looking glass? Loving the self, accepting the self, and finding the sacredness of self - this is where this book really begins.

Breaking free from society trained conventions is not easy by any means. Despite our instant society, there are no quick fixes for this problem. However, once we realize that an unbalanced emphases on externals is a type of bondage for the sexes, races, and creeds, we have taken the first important step. It is long past time to move away from the mindset that categorizes individuals by color or physical appearance to an outlook that recognizes everyone as part of one world, one home; the Earth. Then too, and more importantly, we need to recognize each person as a part of the Divine spark and creation itself.

We are sacred; our bodies are sacred, and the Old Ones did *NOT* create emotional or physical garbage — humanity seems quite apt at doing that all by ourselves. Somewhere along the way we lost sight of this truth. Each person has the right to redefine their sense of self according to spiritual terms instead of societal ones. This is where your beliefs and inner fortitude can begin to help.

Positive New Age living provides ways to redefine our

terminology in a non-judgmental, life-affirming manner. By looking inside ourselves with a different focus and finding beauty there, we can also learn to discern this elusive quality in others — the core personifying the best of what they can be — burning within them. They, like you, are a holy creation.

With this in mind, we should gently remind ourselves that our ways of communicating to, and thinking about, ourselves and others can effect self images dramatically. Words have tremendous power to heal or hurt, which makes a very good argument for honoring the old adage of thinking before we speak or act. If you don't think this is true, just observe a child who has been told regularly that they are "bad" and see what behavior manifests itself.

Similarly, in the quest to define the Sacred Self we need to adjust our awareness to see how preconceived notions effect our interactions. I hate to admit it, but often I find myself being innately less trusting of people outside my own race. Yet, when I think back on negative experiences in my life, it has not been other cultural groups deceiving me, but those I blindly trust because we *LOOK* alike! I hazard to guess that I am but one of many people to discover similar subconscious reactions that have not always been for my betterment.

It is for these aforementioned reasons that we have to begin retraining our minds with more tolerant, one-world outlooks. We can not randomly heed the media, our society, and even sometimes our own negative experiences in judging others. This does not mean throwing out the baby with the proverbial wash water, and tossing caution to the winds with our wisdom. It means, instead, giving every person you meet an opportunity to express their uniqueness, their Sacred Self, then basing your words and actions accordingly. Listen carefully to the music of their distinctive soul as it mingles with your own, and see if harmony can't be found there.

This also doesn't mean that walking a metaphysical path somehow makes all our other social problems disappear. Spiritual pursuits are but one part of a much larger picture. As we search out the face of the God/dess, we suddenly come back to the face of self; the face of humanity and the face of the world. This is our mirror, our educational tool, and all the emotional roller-coaster rides that go with living are part of that picture. Being *spiritual* doesn't change that; in fact, it emphasizes it, which is exactly why I wrote this book.

Mirror, Mirror is my gift to anyone who has ever felt like they were unattractive, ineffectual or at the mercy of fate's whims. It is for folks, like me, who want to rediscover the meaning of personal sanctity, and reclaim it as a foundation to coping with a fractured society. It is also for people who are tired of stereotypes and the hundreds of excuses humankind has devised to justify the often barbaric treatment of those considered "different" and the ravaging of our planet.

Reflecting on the Sacred Self, and rediscovering that being, ultimately returns us to very simple foundations. We begin with a pilgrimage toward wholeness — the wholeness found in knowing ourselves; the wholeness of body, mind and soul in harmony. The path of wholeness and beauty is then walked gently, day-by-day, until it manifests, empowering our reality.

Next, accepting our sacredness also means trusting our

spiritual talents and using those abilities to heal ourselves and our ailing planet. For this step to occur, many pious arguments must get set by the wayside in favor of united action; humankind working together so that earth's beauty and sacredness is likewise maintained. Then, if we're persistent and very fortunate, our children will learn tolerance and vision as the key that opens the door to sacred actualization for our entire species.

In effect, wholeness is a life-long journey that is achieved every day, every moment when we say "We are alive, We are important, We are Divine." I pray this book will help you on this tremendous journey.

One:
Culture, Appearances and History

"Beauty of style and harmony, grace & good rhythm depend on simplicity."

— Plato

"The soul take nothing with her to the other world but her education and culture."

— Socrates

History is an important foundation to changing our perspectives about ourselves and our world. To assure the continuance of our race and this planet, we hope not to repeat the mistakes and atrocities of our ancestors. The best prevention against this I know of is education. In this case, we are reeducating ourselves about what beauty really is, and how our ideas of beauty developed.

From the Mona Lisa to modern love songs, the influence of beauty's spirit lingers on the edge of our awareness. While the effect of idealistic beauty has not always been positive influence, the essence behind it is a powerful one. In our quest for wholeness, both of these facets need to be examined, then positively interpreted for a new, and very different era.

While this examination is not exclusive to the struggle

between the sexes, but it is a very important part of the overall problem. As little as ten years ago a man revealing sadness was not observed as sensitive. Instead he was usually ridiculed, his emotions being interpreted as a hindrance to fulfilling an "appropriate" masculine role. Somehow, our society misinterpreted emotion for weakness, and compassion for gullibility with very painful results. Similar misinterpretations, with variations depending on the generation involved, continue to this very day.

The delineation of what is "appropriate" or "attractive" for each person is changing rapidly on the heels of technology. We talk about liberation freely, yet to watch a normal afternoon commercials you wouldn't know it. The sleek female body is still employed to sell almost everything. Men's muscles are displayed like hardened sculpture in macho environments. You hardly ever see a "normal" looking person featured, and if you do they are often portrayed as somewhat gawkish. These characterizations discourage a one-world mindset, discourage equality, discourage diversity and flaunt sex as the answer to just about anything. Yet, we are not the first generation to experience this problem.

For example, pleasure posters and calendars with scantily clad women appeared during 1920's. The women who broke free of the puritanical mold long enough to shed a few bits of clothing were regarded by most as a lesser species. They were exploited by production companies and ostracized by their families for such impropriety. What image of Sacred Beauty did these women carry, and after all the struggle did they ever find lasting peace at least in their own minds? We may never know.

And for the men who enjoyed these portraits, should they feel guilty for appreciating the feminine form? I don't think so. When exploitation took place it was most often not the consumer at the pinnacle. Yet, we still find ourselves pigeon-holing a man who likes Playboy as automatically being chauvinistic or over-sexed. Does that make a woman who enjoys the same journal automatically a lesbian? Certainly not, but we have to begin realizing just how deep and affecting these types of assumptions can be in all our interpersonal relationships. Confining ourselves to certain images as being essential parts of our feminine or masculine nature obstructs the blending of these two facets into a unified, whole person. This illustration stresses another important point too. Hundreds of excuses have been used down through the centuries to alienate, denigrate and eventually subdue anyone who was considered "different." Like it or not, the traps some of those stereotypes set still ensnare us, quite unwittingly. Sexes, races and creeds are all victims of the patriarchy. It is not just a "woman's issue."

So, as we look for prototypes of sacred beauty in each other, or in the pages of history, we must recognize that this shining being is not without shortcomings. Some of these failings have been brought about by life itself, and others by society. Even so, recognizing that imperfection helps our quest for internal beauty to be more realistic.

It is funny that sometimes the children among us, or even

those considered "backwards" frequently have the answers we lack. Certain tribal cultures in Africa and the West Indies don't consider a woman truly beautiful until she is over 40 because by then, she is wise. In these simpler societies, the knowledge and ability of a person is more essential to survival than externals. Now, to me, this is a tremendous example of what Sacred Beauty could be for all of us, if we would let it.

Historical Overview

We are not, by any means, the first civilization to have awkward ideas about beauty and self worth. As you read the history that follows in this chapter, however, please remember that some chronicles are opinionated, often written by the victorious party. Other portions of history were shared through oral tradition, which can lose much in the translation no matter how adept the linguist. Other segments still have been purposely tainted to suppress groups or individuals deemed inappropriate at that moment.

Thus, historical research is not a perfect study, but one to undertake using as much discernment as possible. Somewhere among the myriads of information available are subtle hints that define the difference between what each book says, what is implied and what likely really happened. This is why the older diaries have become so important to contemporary analogical studies. They are slowly dissolving some of the myths carefully built by politicians and leaders in order to paint a more idealistic picture.

Historians have left us numerous examples that illustrate

both the light and the dark faces of this spirit called Beauty. Many cultures' claim to the term "civilization" was founded in its attention to cosmetic arts, dress, fashion and refinement in same. While the earliest humans took little notice of dress, slowly coverings became practical to ease the uncomfortable effects of the environment.

As vanity and rivalry grew between humans, so did the modes of external adornment, characterized by the nature of each society. Cultures which exhibited war-like attitudes portrayed this outwardly in fearsome accessories meant to scare their enemy. Wode among the Celtic peoples is one such example. Conversely, peaceful cultures decorated themselves and living spaces in far less harsh angles and colors.

Ornamentation underwent dramatic changes depending on the location and time period being examined. Accompanying these transformations, a metamorphosis was also experienced in the arts, architecture, literature and a myriad of "gentle" pursuits that have enriched humankind. Thus, the spirit of beauty and the humanities walked hand-in-hand. So much was the case that Webster's New World Dictionary still defines art with a passage that reads, "the making of things that have beauty."

Even among early peoples, the source of beauty was examined by some of the greatest minds we have known. The questions for them were very similar to our own. Upon what does beauty depend? What are its components? While some philosophers were swayed by passions, others found beauty in the bold line, or the harmony of form. In the final analysis, the constituents of true beauty depended on personal taste and the native culture of the philosopher, artist or writer recounting the information.

For example, one region where architectural masterpieces stand as a lasting memorial to honor beauty is Egypt. Within Egyptian tombs, carefully carved stone reveals hundreds of faces depicting mothers and daughters. These figures line the inner sanctum as an eternal reminder of these women's importance and achievements during life. Among the upper class, the accompanying mummies received garments and jewelry to assure their happiness in the afterlife.

Belly dancing as an art probably had its origins in this region as either a fertility rite or a means to prepare women for childbirth around the same time. In modern Egypt, it remains an integral part of almost all important observances including weddings. Here, the belly dancer is not a sexual object, but the ultimate grace of the feminine principle in movement and form, and her talents are valued highly.

Cleopatra's court (51-49 B.C.) also exemplified the Egyptian ideal of beauty, being likened by contemporaries to rival that of Venus herself. The Egyptian perception of loveliness was repeated with minor variations by the Babylonians, Persians, Chaldeans, and Phoenicians. Some of these groups even managed to better the Egyptian style, which created a kind of battle of vanity between cultures. Slowly, for these regions, beauty became less a matter of reflecting a societal pattern, and more a matter of "keeping up with the

Jones's." Looking at the world today, it is evident that some human habits are very slow to change. The classical Egyptian style also carried over into Greece and Rome. The carvings in this region shows a truly refined eye. In both regions, there was a unique dichotomy of art, some being very realistic, and other pieces portraying the ideal. Neither approach was considered less attractive. It was simply two ways of displaying the same individual or item from different vantage points; the first with the human eye, the second with the eyes of spirit.

Above and beyond all else discussed with regard to beauty, the physical form stands out as popular food for thought. Pythagoras, a Greek philosopher of the sixth century B.C., was determined to discover beauty for what it was. He went so far as to travel to Egypt in hopes that the "parent" civilization could lend some insight. Little did he know that the Egyptians probably looked to some older source for inspiration too!

From these travels, Pythagoras determined that the ideal of beauty was but a foundation to form and structure. This foundation creates a potential of loveliness in all things. It was a divine quality, an ancient mystery, which was content to remain somewhat elusive. With this theory, new thoughts regarding the internal nature of beauty began to form.

Pliny the Elder, a Roman scholar (A.D. 23-79), pondered this aspect, and often came up wanting. Expression, carriage, posture, intellect, and sentiment were all believed to modifying external impressions. Then there were those individuals who defied all visual logic by radiating internal beauty to the point where the externals became secondary. Herein is the quality of beauty, the spirit, that this book really seeks to uncover.

The Greeks were almost infamous for their perceptions, depictions and musings on beauty. Therefore, a little more space will be dedicated to them here. But exactly what was it that lead to their acclaim in this arena? Perhaps, as we have already seen from Pythagoras, it was the fact that the Greeks defined ideal beauty in more esoteric terms.

For them, beauty defied all natural law and moved only in the outer worlds where genius dwells. The Greeks surrounded themselves with this ideal by perfecting their arts, music, literature, and perhaps most notably, their sculptures. The statues of Greek Deities were said to enchant the world with the power of beauty they embodied.

This brings us to another important point. The Greek concept of beauty was also successful in part due to their rich mythology. From the beloved daughter of Jupiter and Dione who became the Goddess of beauty and love, to Venus the image of sexual perfection, Apollo the ultimate man, to the Muses who embodied flawless arts, every portion of Greek fables were permeated with beauty's pattern. True, the Greek Gods and Goddesses were anything but perfect. Nonetheless, their worshipers zealously sought lifestyles that emulated the beauty reflected in mythological tradition.

Moving to a slightly different environment, we can take a brief intermission to ponder oriental thought. Writings from China and Japan are filled with metaphysical illusions of beauty. Yet exactly how this manifested in Eastern culture is uncertain. On one hand we find the binding of women's feet and the intricate layering of clothing. On the other, we have texts and paintings with seemingly modern displays of eroticism. Herein, culture defined beauty and sensuality in a manner befitting to, but not necessarily healthy for, that region.

Perhaps some of the most tenacious people with regard to self care in early history were the Hebrews. The sacred texts of the Old Testament carefully detailed everything from diet to the appropriate maintenance of the body. Even though religious leaders dictated this approach, it reflects a deep abiding belief that the body was sacred and not to be defiled.

The priests of the Hebrew temples had various accoutrements revealing the importance of their station including a fine metal breastplate encrusted with semi-precious jewels. They also wore bells on their robes, which were woven into the edges from sturdy materials. The populace took a que from their leaders, mirroring these styles, especially with pieces of jewelry as a portable treasure and garnish.

The love of adornment for beautification was but one faction of the Jewish toilet, however. More importantly, hair was a central concern. For the ancient Jewess it was a crowning glory. For an elder, the beard was a sign of wisdom. Both were anointed with perfumed oils and cared for with tenacity. Almost in tribute to this important beautifying factor, the professions of barber, hairdresser and perfumer were quite commonplace throughout the Hebrew nations just shortly after the death of Moses. Even Solomon (10th century B.C.) was not immune to the effects of external modifications, especially those of scent. In the Old Testament he says that perfumes and pomades "rejoice the heart."

Not all Hebrew leaders, especially the later Old Testament prophets, were so congenial to these exhibitions of prideful luxury. Isaiah (8th century B.C.) and Jeremiah (7th and 6th century B.C.) both expounded the evils of such adornment. Except for the truly devout, however, their words fell on deaf ears. The Jewish tradition of beauty and personal care was long established, and was carried mindfully into every region in which they settled.

Less in the realms of antiquity, let's move now to the Middle Ages; a time full of both wonders and atrocities. Most women during this period were nothing less than slaves to fashion. The boned bodices that literally suffocated many, were used to accentuate the positive despite their dangers. Likewise, when pregnancy was fashionable, large houpelands (basically cloth bags with a high belt) abounded.

This particular period in history was one of true divergence. The social structure afforded great opulence to the nobles and tremendous poverty to the working gentry. When someone could afford a little luxury, it was always purchased in accordance with prevalent style as a guide. Be it the rather comical beaked shoes with bells, or a huge cod piece during the Elizabethan period (A.D. 1500's), the fashion bug controlled the guidelines for beauty and propriety during these years.

While we generally consider the people of the Middle Ages as lacking in cleanliness, the public bath in certain areas (specifically France) was quite popular. Pope Adrian (A.D. 1100) even recommended that the clergy bathe daily while singing praises. This was also the period when the white-porcelain face became classical.

In sharp contrast to these ideal thoughts and actions, the 11th-13th Centuries brought the Crusades. While the goals for the Crusades at the highest level of the Church was greed, many who participated probably did so with good hearts. The spirit of Beauty in part belongs to the Divine, and as such it was a message that the devout wanted to spread. Unfortunately, the bloody times which followed were anything but holy or beautiful. On a more positive note, the Crusades did open up valuable merchanting routes, specifically with near-Eastern sources. These sources later became important figures in the world of beauty.

Medieval Arabic traders with exotic goods carefully laced each item sold with a healthy dose of magical lore to improve its value. Thus, the price of, and appreciation for, perfumes was raised to a new height. People, especially nobles, carried all manner of sweet bags to protect themselves from sickness and to ensnare romance. This bit of history illustrates the first vestiges of clever "advertising." Even at this early juncture, good "P.R." shaped people's beliefs and created folk traditions that lasted well into modern times.

The Middle Ages were not without their philosophers and thinkers on the topic of beauty. St. Austin taught that true beauty was found in unity. De Crousaz claimed it was in variety and proportion. Then, the Italian schools of painting combined these two ideas to say that beauty's essence blended variety with unity. In reality, all three were neither wrong nor correct in their observations.

During the 1600's one of the wonders of the world, the Taj Mahal, was built by the Mughal emperor Shah Jehan to honor the great wisdom of his wife and companion, Mumtaz. The building was designed as a reflection of Mumtaz's beauty in his eyes, but more importantly it exhibited her importance as a sagacious companion. In this instance the spirit of beauty was given a physical abode at which all humankind would marvel.

In the 1700's, Immanuel Kant, a great German philosopher began expounding on his ideas about beauty. To him, this characteristic was dependent on its ability to please the senses in some manner. Yet, even he found it difficult to express exactly what beauty is. Theorists in every era seemed more adept at telling us where beauty can be found, rather than providing a sound definition. Kant went on to say that perhaps beauty was a universal principle that pervades nature and somehow touches the heart of humankind; a reasonably safe supposition.

Unfortunately Mr. Kant was living in difficult times for such a gentle voice to be heard. The general atmosphere of social unrest coupled with war and high taxation, ravaged the lands and hearts of many. The inquisition witnessed the deaths of thousands of Hebrews in the name of God, along with a few other "undesirables." Afterwards, fear, not beauty, became central to the minds of everyone. Each group wondered who would be targeted next.

Then came the witch hunts of Salem, preceded by the loss of thousands of lives across the European continent during the Witch mania. All this slaughter due to trepidation, misconceptions, and the successful use of the name of God to promote same. Most of those killed were women, and yet what were their heinous crimes?

The wise crone cured animals and villagers robbing the church of some of its power, but more importantly, its gold. The beautiful young maiden sometimes caused a man's eye to stray — nay, this could not have been HIS fault! Hundreds of other accusations flew and with them came more senseless deaths. While innocent people littered the pyre, being forced to admit to devil worship and hundreds of atrocities to please the judges, the church grew in power by controlling through fear. At the same time the validity of women even having a soul was seriously questioned.

There was no intimations of sanctity to be found in these years, no holiness, only horror. While I'm certain there were loving, just people living during these years who anguished over the killing, they could do little to stop the momentum. To step forward would have meant death for them too. Someone had to be left behind to remember the inhumanity.

It would take a miracle for Sacred Beauty to rise from these ashes and evidence itself in Victorian society. Yet somehow a certain sense of holiness did appear. Yes, it was repressive and prudish, but at least in this setting the body was regarded as a Divine gift. Propriety reigned in a manner befitting Emily Post and, and women still remained somewhat in the shadows of their family. Nonetheless, interesting changes were taking place.

The war moved many wives and mothers into a new role as both homemaker and breadwinner without seeming to disrupt the congruity of the family unit. Under the guise of serving the country, women were accepted into the work place, albeit somewhat grudgingly.

It was during this era that the post-Raphaelite artists and writers reflected a refreshing, uplifting air in their work. Paintings blossomed with romance, elegance and magnificent scenes of what was considered the most perfect of creations; nature. Writing focused on whimsical, sentimental themes enriching each diary and library shelf. It was as if a sensitive and idealistic symphony of music began around 1880, setting the tone for the next forty years. This music, filled with Sacred Beauty, helped build the strength of families, villages and the United States.

To the modern mind Victorians were too prim, proper and pristine. You would never know it to look at their bedrooms! These were likened to gilded dens of passion, where many sorted affairs took place. Additionally, the Victorian novels were anything but conservative. These were the years when old taboos for genders were being broken faster than most fine china. The womens' movement started taking shape alongside well-known organizations such as the

SPCA and the Theosophical Society. The long-term effects of these changes are still being felt (and sorted out) in our lives today.

It is difficult to say what happened after 1920 that caused so much confusion and chaos with regard to sacred beauty. War, the Stock Market Crash, crime and other natural progressions of our civilization was like a slap in the face to a naughty child. Suddenly the US was thrust into international matters. With such growth, movement, and the changing needs at home, traditional roles continued to evolve. Various factions disdained this progression, causing yet more confusion, even in the minds of liberal thinkers.

The days of Ozzie and Harriet were upon us, reflecting from the TV to the world what was expected of the family. Beauty was reflected in the way you maintained your role; men working, women dutifully at home, children well behaved and properly dressed. In reality, this image was impossible for some people to secure. More children were conceived out of wedlock, more families were separated by miles, and many women found themselves without husbands to help them care for the home and children thanks to war.

Now, we are talking about our parents, or people born shortly thereafter whose struggles to understand the transforming culture are quite apparent to anyone who takes the time to look. I know my father believed a man didn't outwardly exhibit his emotions. Instead he showed his love by being a good bread-winner and through gifts.

Then there are my sisters, who lived through the era of

picketing, sit-ins, bra burning, Woodstock and hippies. Yet, they are like night and day; one being still very much a creative, free spirited flower child and another a professional nurse. My mother gave them a strong sense of independence, and the rather flurrysome activities of the 60's probably produced some interesting personality traits. Yet, with the ideal of "free love" spreading, I wonder what measure of Sacred Beauty was being instilled in the general public.

This is not an easy question since the non-conformists of the time were actually very tailored within their own ranks. The jargon, dress and ways of communicating were either "in" or "out", leaving little room for true rebels. I feel that the 1960's were a microcosm for many social transitions, where the very group proposing a movement away from the "norm" slowly becomes the "norm" until some other movement sweeps it away.

In the 1920's, the fight was for women's right to vote and smoke cigarettes. In the 1970's and 1980's the discussions centered around equal pay, better jobs and an individual's right to govern their own body. In other words, the struggle to discover sacred beauty and its meaning has always co-existed with the struggle to reform outmoded patriarchal ideals. We just didn't recognize that social upheaval also reflects a spiritual outcry for sanctity, equality and justice.

It should be mentioned, however, that the feminist focus has not always been a positive influence on sacred beauty either. In the race for equality a certain vision of what it means to be male or female, in the spiritual sense, sometimes gets lost. Gentility does not have to mean weakness, nor does strength have to mean crass behavior. We do not have to force ourselves into awkward, unrealistic roles to achieve self worth. We do not have to perform in specific manners just for the sake of appearances.

As children, our image of sacred beauty is intimately linked with the future and our aspirations. We aren't afraid to dream or reach for the stars. Somewhere during late adolescence, we loose our confidence and often adapt an unhealthy attitude that says: "I'm only one person, so what can I do?" Much of the problems surrounding our society can be unearthed in that sentence.

The minute we stopped believing in each individual's ability to change even a small part of the world, a conviction which our Victorian ancestors held dear, we also mislaid the power to do just that. With the loss of that spark, much of our sense of self importance dies. It's time to find those embers once more.

Now, that I have become a parent, I view the attempt to uncover sacred beauty differently, and think about the way this person is presented to my son. For better or worse, I share with him the true me — no gongs, squeaks or bells — just mom. Even more than this, though, I don't discourage his wishful reflections. Somewhere amidst those youthful flights of fancy a really wonderful person can be discovered; a person not afraid to trust in his dreams or himself. This is one way we can begin to make the change towards true beauty and true holiness, by allowing it to be born in our youth.

In our world, we are thankfully beginning to move back towards a vision of the Divine that portrays all people in a positive manner. The Maiden, Mother and Grandmother stand proudly, hand-in-hand with the Son, Father and Grandfather. Together they create a yin-yang balance that grants tremendous freedom and power. One only need to look at New Age artistic endeavors for evidence of this truth.

People are discovering how to express sacred beauty through their medium. They are finding a refreshed vision of Divinity and manifesting it in a way that benefits everyone. It is important to realize, however, that this ability is not limited to a special few; it is everyone's spiritual birthright.

Sacred beauty is not a hopeless cause to be haphazardly abandoned due to laziness or apathy. The struggles we experience today are planting the seeds of awareness in humanity as a species. Slowly those seeds will grow until they overcome conflicts through the resulting transformation.

This will not happen over night, but with each person striving towards harmony within and without, we can create a future filled with lasting loveliness. We can reclaim our Sacred Beauty, honor the sacredness of others, and reclaim the sanctity of our world.

It can begin today with you.

Two:
The Practicum

"The universe is change;
our life is what our thoughts make it."

— Marcus Aurelius

"Tis peace of mind, lad, we must find."

— Theocritus

History, as explored in the last chapter, has been both kind and harsh to the ideal of individual sanctity. We cannot return to change the past. Today and tomorrow, however, are moments within our grasp. The question is, how will we engage them? We can choose to cope with the images we've been given and simply muddle through. Or, we can decide to revolutionize those portraits, and give our Divine perspectives expression.

In a very real sense, this is a self actualization₁ workbook meant to help you define and depict your Sacred Self as it pertains to your reality. I designed this text to inform, challenge and provide thoughtful reflections, including exercises that help facilitate change. While no book can be the perfect guide to personal transformation, it is a place to start.

25

Add your own determination and insight generously to these pages for greatest success.

The search for internal sacredness is, for the most part, a solitary ordeal. Sometimes the going gets rough, and other times it feels like we're getting nowhere. Remarkably, it is in these same moments that some of the most astounding personal transformations occur, often without our knowledge. So, one of the key words for this entire book is **TENACITY!** Don't give up on yourself or your ability to revolutionize your own life.

Before moving into more specifics, let's take a brief look at the questions most readers have when purchasing a self-help text. Below are the most common ones, and answers as they pertain to these pages. Please take a moment to read this section. It will make this book more personally effective and useful.

1. **Who was this book written for?** Everyone and anyone who finds their self esteem being bantered about by commercial "hype." Sacredness is a universal concept. In this book, beauty is not presented as an external commodity, but as an internal reality that everyone can achieve.

2. **Why should I perform the exercises?** Just like exercising your body, your spirit and mind need to work-out on a regular basis. The activities in this book were designed to stress the important points of the text on a conscious and subconscious level. They help redirect your focus toward the

process of change. Fresh ideas and outlooks starts within. Exercises help us assimilate these characteristics, then manifest them outwardly.

If there is something about a particular activity that makes you uncomfortable, by all means make appropriate alterations! Your heart is the most faithful guide in mapping your Path to wholeness. You do not have to continue floating on life's sea accepting every wave that comes along. This is *your* life. Become an active participant in your future reality, starting NOW. Stand up, get creative, and discover your own way to tame the surf!

3. **What tools will I need to perform the activities?** For the most part, only yourself and a few common household items. Each of the exercises includes an introductory paragraph detailing what, if anything, you need before starting. Again, I must stress that if anything about the activity feels awkward, either change it or don't do it. This book will be useless if you're too busy feeling self-conscious to really focus on your goal. You can always return to an exercise later and try it again.

Additionally, I suggest getting yourself a blank diary to track your progress$_2$. Mark your feelings in these pages before and after an exercise. Make notes of stray thoughts that catch your attention. Write down your dreams, or an inspiring quote you stumble across in the newspaper. Carry this diary with you everywhere and allow it to become a reflection of the new person you're becoming.

In the beginning, review your diary once a week. Do this for four weeks. Then, over the next year, review it once a month from beginning to end. I think you will be surprised to discover how much you have changed, grown, and the amount of intuitive insight you possess.

We tend to get so busy with the daily grind that we never see our own progress. Several sections throughout this book have excerpts from my own diary. Re-reading and scanning it for this effort revealed much that I overlooked in previous years. Making your own spiritual diary offers you the same opportunity. Within those pages you can observe, with your own eyes, just how much difference you have made in your life through perseverance.

4. **When and where should I perform the activities?** Any quiet place (unless another location is suggested in the reading) is a good location for introspection. You do not want to be disturbed by unexpected guests, phones, pets or even mates during such intimate moments, so make arrangements for privacy.

Also, if you are ill, angry, or otherwise distracted, hold off on the activity for a while. When our emotions run amok, spiritual pursuits usually fall flat because our attention is elsewhere. When our bodies are in poor conditions, the energy we would normally use for spiritual growth is attending to physical needs. Waiting until you are well rested, healthier or calmer will almost always yield better results.

5. **What am I trying to accomplish in these exercises?**
That is a question only you can answer. Each activity herein
has a specific goal. Nonetheless, they may have different
applications when tailored to suit your needs more directly.
If you're goals for an exercise are different than those
presented, that's fine. A specific personal purpose is
suggested, however, to better focus your valuable time and
energies.

6. **If the exercises don't work, then what?** There are any
number of reasons why a particular activity doesn't function
well. These reasons include:
  — being out of sorts when performing the activity.
  — not taking the time to personalize the activity.
  — the activity had little relative symbolism to you.
  — the need to take more time performing the activity.
    Being rushed or getting interrupted can dramatically
    lessen the level of success achieved.
  — needing more practice at meditation, visualization and
    centering before going on to more advanced
    workings.

If an exercise does not work after trying it three times and
personalizing it, skip it for now and move on. The
progression of this book may be different than the way your
spirit naturally grows and learns. If this is the case, you can
come back to an activity later and have it be very successful!
When all else fails, I have included Chapter 9 ("The

Butterfly of the Soul") at the end of this book to help those who find their development lagging. The suggestions there should alleviate the majority of common stumbling blocks.

7. **What happens when I finish an activity?** When you do master various steps of reclaiming sacred beauty, take the time to reward that progress. All too often we neglect the one person in this world we can always depend on; ourselves. Trying your best and succeeding is something for which to thank yourself.

A grateful spirit doesn't have to manifest spectacularly to be meaningful. Treat yourself to some frozen yogurt, sleep late on a Saturday, or rent a favorite movie. Reinforce your value as a person, and the value of every effort you put forth in becoming self-actualized. Little acknowledgments like this reinforce personal, positive energy so we can walk the Path of Beauty confidently.

> *"Be sure to keep a mirror always nigh*
> *In some convenient, handy sort of place*
> *and now then, look squarely in thine eye*
> *and with thyself keep ever face-to-face"*
> — John K. Bangs

Three:
Through The Looking Glass

"Life is the mirror of king and slave."

— Mary Ainge DeVere

Earlier in the twentieth century there was an on-going debate in psychology regarding the belief that people are fundamentally alike. Freud saw Eros as the binding motivation in all human interactions, while Adler believed the true motivator was power. Existentialists, like Fromm, viewed the human creature as seeking only after self.

When Carl Jung came on the scene, he offered a completely different outlook. In his philosophy, individuals are dramatically different in elemental ways, while archetypal instincts motivate them from within. This concept shattered the psychological world, even though it was thousands of years old. Hippocrates himself discussed various human temperaments as types,[3] never ignoring the wonders of diversity in his writings.

It is from this seething mass of hypotheses that the modern thinkers draw certain conclusions. Spiritually speaking, I stand with Jung and Hippocrates, voting for humankind's uniqueness. This book is based on the notion that each soul is a totally atypical creation. That same soul is linked by its originating spark to the Creator-Spirit, thus it is immutable. Yet, in the scheme of every-day life, how many of us regard ourselves as part of that Universal scheme or as a wholly original individual?

How Do I See Myself?

"While Aristotle called beauty a 'gift from God,' Socrates called it a 'short lived tyranny;' Theophrastus, a 'silent deceit;' Theocritus, an 'ivory mischief'."

— Diogenes Laertius

Look to the mirror and what do you see? The grey hair sneaking around your face, a wrinkle or two, a nose slightly off center? Or, do you instead see a shining spirit, whose shell may not be "perfect" by society standards, but is certainly still a marvelous creation?

In the quest for your Sacred Self, first consider why you feel appearances are important. In a brief review of human interactions, it seems that the preoccupation with externals developed around the same time as our sense of individuality. Ancient cultures devised various personal care products and tools to primp, allure, please and tease (see Chapter 1). So, realistically, we come by our "hang-ups" quite honestly.

The desire to be appreciated and stand out from the crowd is something almost inherent to the human nature. We need to know that we are unique; that we have a face and a name worth remembering. As the numbers of humans on this planet grew, the need to express our individuality likewise grew. Now we are faced with overcrowded cities, each of which is filled with people who could benefit greatly by running to a roof and shouting "I AM!"

I AM! This powerful, affirming phrase repeats its nature through hundreds of ancient philosophies. In the Bible it says, "be still and know I AM..." The Tibetan chant of OM means, I AM. Again and again we, alongside our ancestors, have raised our voices to cry, searching earnestly for ways to tell ourselves that we really exist, that we really are important. All our attempts at external changes will not grant us this assurance. It is born from within.

Each day of living is an open door. What lies just beyond the threshold is determined by a number of factors, including your outlook, actions, motivations and daily routine. Of all these things, a positive personal attitude is one of the most important to successful living.

We all know the notion of like attracting like. Have you ever noticed that pessimistic people tend to have more 'coincidental' difficulties than optimistic ones do, and wondered why? To explain this, visualize the energy each person transmits like one line in a web. This line seeks other lines on the same frequency so they can communicate and mesh. Therefore, someone who broadcasts dark, gloomy moods leaves a little of that ambiance wherever they go, and also draws similar energy back toward themselves. Can you imagine the effects of this in a crowded city where hundreds of people are unhappy?

An article appearing in the July 1993 *Wall Street Journal* discussed the mental and physical abuse of women in lower class urban environments. The author observed that the reason for this inhumanity was the power of one type of energy to breed more of itself. From the drug deals in the streets to the messages presented through certain popular music forms, urban violence is glibly portrayed as the perfect answer to life's inequity along with sexual subjugation.

In high-crime districts, the energy of brutality barges into homes with an attitude that says "if I can get away with it, do it." This is pinnacle of what happens when people stop believing in their power to change themselves. Instead of fighting back, many of these people feel helpless and simply deliver their life into the momentum of the times with horrific results.

By picking up this book, you have expressed a desire to begin fighting back, and to see yourself differently. Discovering your Sacred Self is not something you can do for anyone else. The search must be motivated by a heart-felt yearning to become more than a number, more than what people have typecast, and more than the sum of your experiences. Now you will move forward to reclaim the helm of your life. The first step on this journey is making a promise to yourself, a commitment to try.

A Personal Pledge (Exercise 1)

Initiate your efforts toward rebuilding the Sacred Self with the dawn; the perfect emblem of new beginnings and new opportunities. Some day soon, get up before the sunrise and sit quietly by your window. Watch the world awaken with the eyes of a child. As those first rays of sun touch the land, let them touch your heart to ignite a fire that can not be extinguished. Make a resolution to yourself and the Divine on this day to start your journey towards wholeness.

The form this promise takes is very personal. One person might pray, another might write a letter listing their goals, another might muse silently about their life thus far. What is important here is changing your attitude. From this moment forward you are not one of life's victims, but a co-creator$_4$ with the Great Spirit.

When you leave that window, vow to dump the sociological trained garbage at the sill and start anew. Each time you see the sun, remind yourself of your pledge, and pour vibrant golden energy into a positive outlook that sustains you throughout the day.

Realistic Self Images (Exercise 2)

The Path of Beauty is not always straight or sure. Like any road there are twists, turns and obstructions to be overcome. One of the first of these is dealing with our own, often harsh, judgements of self. Everyone wants to achieve something special in their life; that is natural. What is aberrant is how unrealistic the word "special" often becomes.

To a toddler, a beautiful daisy blooming on a spring day is special. For a five year old having the love and trust of a favored pet is special. Why are adults ideas of what is

35

important and special so drastically different? We can't all be famous or rich, but something in our society makes us feel inadequate without the pomp and circumstance.

There is nothing wrong with having dreams. Actually, they are very healthy. If you berate yourself for not achieving those dreams, however, then it is time to reevaluate how realistic you are being. For example, you can't become a rocket scientist without an education. If that's *really* what you want, your first step is returning to school, not applying for a job where your qualifications will immediately fall short.

Sometimes we get so anxious to fulfill our aspirations that we forget the necessary steps that will bring dreams into reality. Unfortunately when we skip those procedures, we often get discouraged, feel inadequate or give up altogether. At this point, sensibility becomes a valuable friend. Realism does not have to take away your hopes. Instead, it gives you a solid foundation from which to build.

For this exercise you need nothing other than a piece of paper, a writing implement and a little spare time. Find a quite place where you feel no pressure to do anything other than center your attention on yourself. On the paper make a list of what you perceive to be your positive attributes, negative attributes, goals and dreams. Write until you feel as if all your tensions have poured out through your pen.

Now put that paper aside for a few moments and relax. Enjoy the peacefulness that surrounds you before trying to appraise your responses. As you review these lists, you will probably be pleasantly surprised to discover more positive attributes than expected. Most people don't spend much time appreciating their virtues, if they recognize them at all.

Next, when looking at the negatives, see how many you have the power, energy, and wherewithal to change. If you put down being a poor cook as a negative, for example, this could be remedied by spending a little more time in the kitchen. Or, if you are out of shape, an exercise program can get you moving in a constructive direction for physical well-being. In both cases, any progress helps your self esteem greatly because YOU have successfully made an effort towards transformation.

Third, consider what actions could be taken today to bring any one of your goals or dreams into reality. Then get motivated! Life does not serve us. We have to go out and take it by the horns if we want to tame those aspirations.

Finally, keep this list handy. Tuck the paper away somewhere for review in a year. It will become an important tool in gauging your growth. I'm a terminal note-writer who hangs everything up, marking off the completed items and adding new ones as I think of them. But there is something to be said for the element of surprise.

After a year, you'll probably have all but forgotten about that little exercise and discover it in a sock drawer. What a pleasant revelation it is to see negative tendencies decrease or disappear off your list. How exciting it is to see how much closer you are to achieving your goals, if at least one of them hasn't already been accomplished.

Remember, your Sacredness is measured in how you live,

how you treat people, and the joy you get from both; not in notoriety or cash flow.

Personal Diary — January 1993

"When I started writing as a child, I hoped to make it a career. In college, I pursued that dream by taking every English course I could. After graduation, I continued to write stories just for myself or small journals while working as a secretary, thinking any hope of a profession was long gone. Yet not long thereafter an opportunity presented itself, born from a casual conversation between friends. It was only creating and edit a local newsletter, but it was writing. My dream suddenly had a new spark! Four years of constant production work later, a manuscript was born from which my first published book took shape. Now it seems that five books are written, and I hardly know where the time has gone.

In retrospect, I recognize now that all my youthful aspirations didn't come into reality earlier because I didn't have any confidence in my own abilities to write...or to touch lives through that writing. Despite my initial fears and uncertainty, it seems that sometimes there is a "happily ever after" ending for at least one of the scenes in this play called life, but the dress rehearsals were certainly hell!"

Self Affirmations (Exercise 3)

Most people need to remind themselves periodically that they are, indeed, a good person. What we perceive of ourselves is shaped every day and every moment by number of circumstances including job struggles, family squabbles, and misunderstandings between friends. As these situations arise, the strength of our convictions regarding who we are, how we live, and our self worth may waiver. By making self-affirmation a routine, we can keep the inner well of confidence filled and flowing, no matter our situation.

For this activity, your list of positive attributes can be very useful. Compile some simple affirmations from that list. For example, if one of your good characteristics is kindness, the phrase "I am good hearted" might be appropriate. The best part about affirmations is that they can be recited just about anywhere — while shaving, driving, walking or house cleaning.

Affirmations require no tools other than your mind. If need be, they can even be recited silently; thoughts have energy too.

In the beginning, perform affirmations like they were good meals; take them three times a day. After a year, change the frequency to once a day, like a spiritual vitamin supplement.

Affirmations should be fairly short, meaningful and full of power. They should always be phrased in a positive manner, and seem most effective when repeated in sets of three (the number of body-mind and spirit in symmetry). If you happen to be alone and can shout or sing the affirmations, all the better. Volume helps release transformational energy, and a lot of pent up tension besides!

Below are a few good examples of personal affirmations.

Wherever there is a blank, you can insert your name or the word 'I,' but I suggest using your name. There is a lot of strength in the term that has designated your existence since birth — don't be shy about tapping that vibrant energy.

_____ is a holy creation

_____ is strong (or healthy, or happy)

_____ is a co-creator with the Divine

_____ has the power to change his/her life

_____ is beautiful within and without

_____ has fortitude (or tenacity, determination)

_____ is trust worthy (or honest, ethical, honorable)

Besides using affirmations to reinforce positive features you can also employ them to develop new virtues. Every word in any language carries a vibration all its own. Here, you repeat the idea of possessing a quality as an already achieved fact, which accomplishes two things. First, you release the energy of those phrases into your life daily. Secondly, the repetition makes you more consciously aware of trying to develop those characteristics throughout the day.

How Do I See Others?

"Truth is the shattered mirror strewn in myriad bits; while each believes his little bit the whole to own."

— Sir Richard Burton

There is a little Pygmalion in all of us that is tempted to

redesign the universe in our own image. The number of "one true religions" that exist and an exorbitantly high divorce rate are two powerful testimonies for this verity. The snare of the Pygmalion syndrome is feeling that our way of perception, of walking, of *being* is totally correct, and therefore good for everyone around us.

While each religion has managed to sculpt the Divine into a preferred likenesses, people are not so cooperative. Externals, unless transformed by surgery, are indelible. Internals can be changed by external pressures, but forceful disruption of the self leaves noticeable emotional scars. Simply put, you can't assume that others will live up to the expectations you place on yourself. They are not you.

Just as you seek uniqueness and individuality, those around you are also struggling with their own sense of sacredness. They are equally uncomfortable with certain roles that have been thrust upon them. So, as you begin releasing the unrealistic expectations you held for yourself, start unburdening people close to you similarly. Direct your attention to the attributes in them that inspire your love or friendship. Then, allow that feeling to be the key in building tolerance for other traits you find less pleasurable.

This system works well for even those individuals deemed acquaintances in our lives. If the only redeeming value you can find in someone is the color of their socks, then that becomes the focal point of your attention. While we can't honestly like everyone we come in contact with, this perspective helps maintain the best energy possible throughout the most difficult situations.

Affirmation of Others (Exercise 4)

How often have you met a perfectly disagreeable person? You know, those individuals who seem determined to make everyone around them miserable? If you have to work or live with such an individual, you will need to find a coping mechanism.

One approach that can really make a difference is affirming these people, and others who intimately touch your life. We rarely realize how pessimistic our speech patterns become, and how critical many unconsidered phrases sound. By taking a little extra time for forethought in communications, we can successfully turn a negative into a positive.

For this exercise, find one person who could really use an emotional boost. Spend an entire week making a fuss over everything they do for you (or someone else). These comments should not be forced. Instead, simply make a conscious effort to be more aware of their beneficial deeds, no matter how minor.

This exercise engenders two things. First, you will discover how often you overlook the nice, little things people do for you. Secondly, after a week you should begin to notice subtle changes in the individual you've been affirming. They may be happier, less tense, more friendly or even more organized because their confidence has been strengthened.

What a tremendous blessing it is when we can support each other and learn in the process!

Personal Diary — June 1992

"Things at the office seem to have gone from bad to worse. The Dragon Lady takes every opportunity to gossip about me or reprimand any efforts I make toward meeting her half way. My frustration is starting to show in my work, and I hate getting up in the morning. Since it's obvious this woman is not going to change for my sake, perhaps I need to change the way I look at this whole matter to make it livable....."

(Three Entries Later)

"Well the bandage seems to have worked somewhat. I have made the extra attempt to be kind, courteous and supportive of the dragon lady. About her only good quality is that she's a dedicated mother, so I have tried to use that to build the lines of communication between us. Amazingly enough, she actually said thank you today. I know in my heart that she is not much different than before, and I certainly don't trust the situation, but at least it is easier to contend with for 8 hours a day than it was before..." [6]

But what about irritating or unhealthy habits and other personality features that make social interaction difficult? Certainly we should also work on remedying these. One would not allow a child to run across the street without a proper reprimand to inspire learning. Similarly, if the people close to us are participating in the quest for transformation, sharing constructive observations can be very helpful.

It's much easier for folks to accept criticism from those they perceive as knowing them intimately. Keep your words gentle and reassuring, and offer to help in any way you can. This way, people who care for each other become support beams in the building of a renewed, vital Sacred Self.

Collaborate & Change (Exercise 5)

For this activity, you and a partner sit down and specify one aspect of your own personality that you want to change. Also designate a feasible time frame in which to achieve that goal. Then, both individuals promise to sensitively help the other in achieving their transformation. This way, neither person feels picked on or singled out, and they have a built-in cocoon to help protect and support them through the difficult spots.

At the end of the time period, meet again to celebrate your progress and any measure of success. If change hasn't been quite as fast in coming as you expected or hoped, use this meeting to agree on an extension. Our perceptions of how long personal transformation takes are typically impractical. This is a learning process. Even discovering that you've expected too much, too soon, is an excellent lesson for which to be grateful.

How Do Others See Me?

"The best mirror is an old friend."

— George Herbert

Another question in our reflections about the Sacred Self is not only "why" appearances are important but *what* appearances are important. For example, one would not consider wearing a bathing suit or pajamas to a job interview. Conversely, while neatness counts, a prospective employer's personal preferences regarding appearance should not influence our chances for employment. Unfortunately, nearly everyone has some subconscious level of response to outward beauty, whether they like it or not.

So how do we as spiritual beings cope with other people's perceptions without compromising our quest for wholeness? First and foremost we must recognize that we all play a myriad of roles in our lives. These roles do not define everything about us; they are only part-time dramas. In cases where the role is an uncomfortable one, we have to find ways to 'take on' and 'put off' that character so that the central being is left intact.

Putting on a Persona (Exercise 6)

For this activity you will need clothes appropriate to whatever scenario in which you feel ill-at-ease. Also find a picture of someone who you feel exemplifies the best implied characteristics of that situation. Check magazines, news-

newspapers, calendars, photo albums, or any other collections that you don't mind disassembling.

Next, sit down and look at the chosen image. Devise one word phrases describing that individual. Say you're having trouble at work. For this exercise, you might choose the portrait of an admired co-worker. In them, you see the qualities of leadership, organization, professionalism, and diplomacy. Make a list of those attributes on a piece of paper and keep it handy.

Next, remove the clothing you are wearing one piece at a time. With each item, remove the unacceptable parts of your personality (for that specific situation). For example, if you've been plagued by carelessness, sloppy work, and poor communication skills, name pieces of your casual attire after those negative aspects. Let each drop to the floor unnoticed and leave them there.

Finally, begin dressing in the appropriate attire. Now, each item of clothing accents the new persona you are building. Name the desired attributes out loud, or envision yourself in the work place performing tasks efficiently.

You are now, and for the rest of the day, a slightly different version of you. That doesn't mean your values are lost, or that fakery is involved. Instead, you have used a common acting technique to prepare yourself for an awkward task. When you come home, leave that persona at the foot of the bed with your clothing just like before.

Repeat this technique any time you feel inadequately prepared to face the conditions into which you're being thrust.

The only word of caution is to remember that this is only a temporary character. End this dramatization once you arrive home, and don't 'put on' a character during the course of relationships. Your home is a sacred space, and relationships are too fragile for that kind of pretense. At the core of whatever personality you devise is the spirit and essence of the Divine. Allow that to be your guide.

Have it Your Way (Exercise 7)

In my own life there has often been an excessive concern about "the sake of appearances." Even today, I hesitate to kiss my husband in public because I didn't grow up that way. The only method I know of to break free of these fabricated restrictions is to literally "cut loose."

So, when the opportunity arises, try taking a step away from the norm. If you are going out with friends, but don't really want to wear make up or a tie, don't! If there's a shirt you absolutely love, but at which your mate grimaces, wear it anyway!

People who truly care about you can show their support and respect by letting you express your individuality freely, without becoming the brunt of jokes. Those who don't know you should simply mind their own business. As long as self expression doesn't hurt anyone, or go beyond mundane law, you have every right to break free of old, worn-out conceptions. Surprise people! Surprise yourself!

Obviously, you don't want to take this exercise too far, like showing up at a four star restaurant in a bikini. Rebellion against internal constraints is best tackled in small, sensible packages. Each success, balanced against common sense, places another feather on the bird of your spirit.

Personal Diary — New Years 1992

"Mitchie has promised today to teach me how to say "it's not my problem." I have been "mom" to many people, even my own age, for a long time. Unfortunately, I'm never that nurturing to myself. The time has come to break free of always being a safe house in the storm. Right now, I'm the one who needs a little sanctity, yet I struggle with feeling selfish.

There are so many things in my life that need tending to. I can't possibly give them the attention they deserve if all my energy is spent trying to solve other folks problems. I guess it's time for the "kids" fly on their own...for me to fly without so much baggage... and a time for me to let both happen."

How Do I See the World?
"And all of their singing was, 'Earth, it is well'!"
— Bliss Carmen

If we expect the worst, we often get it. The spirit of pessimism and apathy has ravaged this planet for the last fifty years. So many shrug their shoulders, feeling unimportant, and numbly perform their daily tasks. Indifference is a terrible enemy to both the Sacred Self and the sanctity of Earth. It hinders growth, inspiration and affirmative action.

Sometimes it seems easier not to care. Apathetic attitudes can become very comfortable; comfortable, that is, until something goes awry and we're looking for someone to blame. I read a quote by a Native American writer whose name I can't recall, but the words were powerful. He said something to the effect that if you feel your foundations shaking, know it is the Spirit shaking you. In other words, it's time to wake up from our spiritual slumber.

You are not at the whims of fate, but the world is not so fortunate. It moves slowly in space, subject to the caprice of its inhabitants. The forecast for humanity as a race, and this home we call Earth is dependent upon the patterns and cycles we build today. Every moment of living is an opportunity to make a positive change for the future.

As we move closer to achieving the goal of sanctification, our connections to this world become more important. The lessons it presents, the magnificence of dew drops and stars, are frequently overlooked amidst the contemporary hustle. Yet, any spiritual progress we make will mean little if we devastate the Earth before sharing the vision of the Sacred Self with our children.

Part of the charge to the spiritual questor is one that requires reciprocity with nature, and service to Gaia in body, mind and spirit. Earth is a living thing; vital and unique. Take the time to extend some of your energies for reformation to the very thing that sustains you and all humankind; this planet.

Positive Action for Earth-Healing (Exercise 8)

As you uplift your self-image and that of others, likewise renovate the representations of Earth. The ecological movement has aided this effort through public awareness. Conversely, sometimes I feel it has highlighted too many of the negatives.

When individuals feel overwhelmed by circumstance they also often feel unable or inadequate to act. Since the human creature was the cause of problems for this planet, we can also be the instrument of healing. This is the message we need to broadcast to our fellows; one of encouragement, refreshed vision and ecological sanity. This serves the mind of Gaia.

On a personal level, positive action can take many forms. From recycling projects at home, to picking up litter at a park and educating our children, every small step is well worth taking. Build these activities into your weekly or monthly routine so that you get closer to nature, and improve its condition at the same time. Here, you serve the body of Gaia.

Finally, for Her spirit another technique is used. Visualizations, prayers, meditations — whatever form your supplications to the Universal Good take, use some of that vibrant power on the Earth's behalf. Envision a world lush and fruitful, where animals are not endangered (including people). Release the energy of well being to a near-by tree, bit of grass, or flowers you tend with your own hands.

As you care for the Earth, you will quickly discover you are caring for yourself too. There is something tremendously inspiring about knowing you have done something to facilitate a better future. Your efforts will combine with those of other caring individuals and slowly, sometimes imperceptibly, improvement comes both for your spirit, and Gaia.

Personal Diary — February 1992

"Today I felt like my efforts were insignificant. I turned on the TV to hear of yet more problems with pollution at NY dump sites. It made me so angry to watch reporters droning emotionlessly on about the health and well being of animals and humans... I just had to get out of the house.

I took a short drive to Niagara Falls and watched for what seemed like an eternity. The water is so beautiful in winter, sparkling with bits of ice and snow beneath the sun. Then it suddenly occurred to me that once this powerhouse was only a little drizzle over a rock in an unnamed stream. Maybe, just maybe, I can learn to be that drizzle!"

Chapter Notes

1. By definition actualization means putting into motion a reality. In other words, the power to change is already a truth within us. It simply needs stimulation to manifest without.

2. These can be purchased at gift shops where greeting cards and stationary are carried for under $10.00. If this proves costly for your budget, try a three ring binder with lots of paper instead.

3. These types were delineated as Sanguine (buoyant and cheerful), Choleric (cantankerous), Phlegmatic (passive) and Melancholic (regretful and despondent).

4. The term Co-creator is part of the New Age ideal which gives each individual responsibility for their actions, or lack thereof. For while "God is in His heaven," we are still on this earth, and everything we do effects the web of life. In this sense, we become partners with the Divine spark to work towards spiritual fulfillment.

5. The Magi Newsletter was produced from my home in Buffalo between 1988 and 1992. It was a magical theme journal dedicated to creativity and tolerance among all faiths.

6. This office situation has since been terminated, not of my choosing. However, the new job that I presently hold is much better and far less stressful. I have come to think that the 'dragon lady' did me a favor by making life miserable there, because the after-life seems like heaven!

Four:
The Mystical Commode

"One self-approving hour whole years outweighs
of stupid starers and of loud huzzah;
And more true joy Marcellus exil'd feels
Than Caesar with a senate at his heels."

— Alexander Pope

"He has half the deed done, who has made a beginning"

— Horace

The lavatory is the place where we primp and hone the external self into a form deemed suitable for public consumption. Here, we wash, check our weight, refine our scents, shave and straighten our collars. Such fussing sometimes positions the human body on equal footing with merchandise going up for bid. Nonetheless, I think there are ways to redeem this time, and employ it more constructively.

The Royal Chamber:
"As men come within the circle of its influence they involuntarily pay homage to that which is the one preeminent distinction; the royalty of virtue."

— Henry C. Potter

53

The word toilet comes from a French term, *toilette*, meaning linen cloth. This stems from even an older Latin word, *texo*, which translates as "I weave." Using these older definitions of the word, the bathroom can become an area where you repair the fibers of your personal sanctity.

Since the modern world already labels this room a "throne," why not take advantage of the symbolism this evokes? In some ways, the lavatory can be a truly regal place. For many individuals, this is the one of the few locations in the house where they are assured of peace and privacy.

On a spiritual and emotional level, treating ourselves once in a while like royalty is very healthy. In our own lives, we are the ultimate rulers — we steer the helm of thought and action, we gather the gold of wisdom, and fashion the laws of the land which is our home. As such, be it a house or apartment, this area is your hallowed ground and should be treated accordingly.

The information I am about to share is applicable in any part of the area you call "home." However, this chapter focuses a majority of attention only the bathroom as a functional space for reflecting upon, and reclaiming, the Sacred Self.

Dedication and Delineation of Sacred Space (Exercise 1)

In every religion I know of, areas considered holy are set apart. Many of these edifices, shrines and groves have an ambiance that is unmistakably hushed and calm. Once within, you sense a unity with all time and a remarkable tranquility.

In this realm there are no expectations — just you and Spirit. That is exactly how sacred space(s) of your own devising should feel.

In this exercise you are going to become your own Priest/ess, administering rites of blessing that will be instrumental in revolutionizing your life. The way each individual approaches this activity should reflect of their own spiritual path. Remember that sacred space can be any area that is dedicated or safeguarded in a manner befitting your faith. What really changes is your attitude toward that region. By performing special rites in your bathroom, you create a sanctuary where the adventure towards wholeness can begin. Best of all, since this room is already somewhat secluded, it lends itself well to the task!

There are many simple techniques to help you along. First, straighten up the room and clean a little. Have you ever noticed how much happier a room seems when it's uncluttered? The energy of your labor changes the atmosphere to one more conducive for spiritual pursuits. After all, I have yet to walk into a messy church! A physically and psychically tidy area is also less distracting.

Next, think about the things from your own religion that help create the sensation of a sacred haven. Are there any prayers you find especially empowering? A song or chant? How about a verse from a poem or favorite book that has deep personal meaning? Find some verbal means of invoking a Divine presence, comfortable to you, and memorize it.

As you close (and lock) the door of the bathroom, you

are terminating your connections to the "outside" world for a few moments. As you pray or meditate, it signals the beginning of your private time of introspection with the Old Ones. A burning candle for inspiration, some incense for focus, or a selection of calm music can all create a distinctive ambiance so that lifeless porcelain suddenly radiates with vibrant, positive energy.

How you utilize this time is really up to you. A long hot shower where all your tensions and worries get rinsed away is one good option. The ritual bath (exercise 3) is another. Or, more obviously, sit on the seat of honor (with the lid down for comfort) and read a few pages in a motivational book. Enjoy the quiet isolation this room offers and the chance to pamper yourself until you feel ready to leave.

Finally, give a word of thanks before opening the door. Once ajar, the energy you created within flows out to your entire house. You emerge as a Holy creation, a sacred space unto yourself where the light of the Divine can always find expression.

Decorations to Encourage Positive Images (Exercise 2)

Small garnishes, carefully chosen for their positive input, are more effective than you might initially suspect. Bright colors, for example, encourage fresh energy, while pastels inspire quiet insight. Plants arouse a stronger connection with nature, and Divine images give us positive portraits of the God-self on which to focus.

Before you begin hunting for significant items to add to

your sacred bath space$_1$, understand that your accents do not have to be overt or expensive. Nor do I expect everyone reading this book to completely remodel their bathroom! In fact, the subtle touches are twice as powerful on a subconscious level, so start out small.

The emotional response you have to your embellishments is of primary consideration. Each item placed in your hallowed area should remind you of personal completeness, encourage self assurance, and bring a smile to your face. I can provide a list of helpful suggestions, but the way you employ each adornment may be quite different than what I suggest. Please follow your instincts. They are a very good friend to which to listen.

Below are some decorating options. In each case, scrutinize the item(s) both for symbolic value and practicality. There is no need to sacrifice utility for metaphysical goals in the quest for the Sacred Self. If anything, this search is a exceptionally sensible endeavor that carefully blends daily living and Spirit into a unified, dynamic whole.

Soaps — Specialty shops and import stores carry soap in all kinds of shapes. For constancy and calm in your life, a good choice might be sea shell shaped soap. For a lovely Goddess image, try cameo carved soap.

The color and scent of the soap also has metaphorical value. I prepare home made soap with specially chosen herbs and color bases, during waxing moons$_2$, to accentuate my goals. With commercial varieties, however, there is no reason not to purchase the soap during an appropriate moon phase instead! Here is a brief list of common color and aromatic associations[3]:

Color : Red, Orange
Scents: Cinnamon, clove, ginger
Attribute: Energy, Power, Purging, Fire, Leadership

Color: Yellow, Orange,
Scents: Lemon, Rosewood,
Attribute: Creativity, Inception, Dawn, Illumination

Color: Green
Scents: Pine, Cedar, Mint
Attribute: Growth & Change, Well-being

Color: Blue
Scents: Lotus, Lily, Lavender
Attributes: Calm, Water, Healing, Nurturing, the Moon

Color: Purple, Violet,
Scents: Rose
Attributes: Spirituality, Wisdom, Non-linear learning

Color: Brown
Scents: Chamomile, Basil, Musk
Attributes: Grounding, Earth, Fertility

Color: Black
Scents: Frankincense, Sage, Myrrh
Attributes: Banishing, rest, Contemplation

Baskets — Hanging baskets hold an assortment of practical, everyday bath items. Combine therein your soaps and scents with a few insightful embellishments for an elegant and useful accessory.

Choose ornamentation for the basket(s) to reflect aspects of your goal, or various spiritual ambitions. A live plant with vines in one basket symbolizes both grounding and growth towards the "light," for example. Dry flowers scented with aromatic oil affixed to the outside of the basket convey their subtle message each time you enter the room. For this illustration dried mint leaf is a good choice.

Similarly, choose the basket's hanger for its color, or even the way it's braided if made from yarn. Two strands of yarn symbolize partnership, while three work better in balancing the body-mind-soul.

Rugs, Towels, Wash Clothes, Shower Curtains, Bath Mats — the interest of not repeating this idea too often, almost all the items listed herein can be picked for your Sacred Bath according to their hue. Also, look at their patterns. Do they make a design that reminds you of something beneficial? Are there pictures or words emblazoned on the surface that inspire good thoughts? To find one or two that suit your higher senses, try second-hand stores and wholesale outlets.

Next, consider their texture. Some individuals react more strongly to tactile input. What feeling does the cloth's weave and nap stimulate? Is it smooth, comforting, and calm? Or, perhaps it is slightly rough to activate alertness?

Shower curtains have scenes or designs which can be very stimulating. For tub mats, I like the self-stick cut outs that you can lay out in meaningful patterns. Runes[4] offer one option here, being easily laid out using flower cut-outs as shown below.

Strength, Warrior energy, Partnership

Realistically, no one can change their bathroom decor to suit every single circumstance in life. Instead, choose a few items with broad-spectrum meanings (love and growth being two good themes). Surround yourself with visions of Sacredness born from your own insight. There is no better place to find Spirit than within.

Towel Racks — When I'm not taking a shower, I like using these as an alternative herb dryer! If you don't happen to by a home herbalist, however, an alternative is making a sachet of herbs and hanging it from the rack. When the room heats up, the herbs naturally release their transformational aroma. One recipe recommended for positive spiritual ambitions is: one teaspoon each of lavender, orange rind, lemon peel, pine needles, ginger, and rose petals. This inspires peace of mind, health, cleansing, purification, energy and love, respectively.

Art & Literature: While not quite as practical as the other suggestions in this section, mindful choices and placement for art can also help your spiritual pursuits. One of the best locations is the back of the bathroom door, or on the wall across from your mirror. There are hundreds of interesting posters that depict everything from the eight fold path of Buddhism to pastoral woodland scenes.

Similarly, almost everyone likes to have a few good books or journals handy here, so why not choose them according to your goals? Read Time or Newsweek when your awareness of the world needs improvement. Or, read books like *Loving the Goddess Within* by Nan Hawthorn when you struggle with self-admiration and confusion over sexuality. This way, every moment spent here is applied in a positive manner!

Thinking about each object placed in the Sacred Bath will improve your understanding of your own vision. Just like assembling a jigsaw puzzle, each time we consider the meaning behind something, we also have to look carefully to our own hearts and lives to see where it fits. Slowly, these pieces start coming together and form a recognizable portrait — the portrait of the REAL person within

Personal Diary — November 1990

"We just moved to a new house... just renting it, but it feels great to have a little more room. When we started moving things in, I discovered the most marvelous bathroom decoration still hanging on the wall. The construction was uncomplicated; some braided yarn, a few silk flowers and a

packet of herbs secured to a ring, but the charm! Despite a layer of dust covering the upper edge, there is something special about that little decoration. I plan to keep it here to remind me that even beneath a sprinkling of dirt, loveliness can be found in the simplest of things."

Luxury Ritual Bath (Exercise 3)

Earlier in this chapter I mentioned the idea of a ritual bath. Water played an elemental role in religion as a medium of blessing and cleansing, most notably seen today at baptisms. This emblematic connection is literally thousands of years old, dating back to some of the earliest folk healers and wise people.

We spend nine months of our earliest lives in a watery domain. Because of this, most humans react very strongly to water imagery, and naturally respond to its caress when anxiety abounds$_5$. The idea behind this exercise is to combine a necessary function (getting clean) with a rite of self-blessing, and a moment of well deserved tranquility.

For some unknown reason the contemporary world often mistakes relaxation for laziness. You will need to overcome that idea to make this activity really worthwhile. With the tensions and hurries these days, "leisure" time may be the best invested moments you ever spend. It renews the spirit so everything you accomplish is achieved without sacrificing personal health and well-being. This is an especially important lesson to those work-aholics out there!

Begin by finding a secure candle holder, a blue-green

candle (for growth and peace), some favorite incense, tranquil music, bubble bath, glitter, some oil of myrrh, and any herbs you enjoy. Bundle the loose herbs into a cheese cloth ball or tea strainer. Begin as you did when you first created your sacred space, by closing the door and leaving the mundane world behind you. Light the candle and turn on the music while filling the bath. Please make sure your tape player or radio is safely away from the bath water.

Envision the water glowing with white-blue light. Add your herbs and the bubble bath so that a rich aroma fills the room. On top of the foam, sprinkle glitter so it appears like the stars are at your feet. Get in and just relax for 5-10 minutes. Breath deeply, in through your nose and out through your mouth, visualizing the light from the water filling every cell of your being. Take care not to fall asleep in the tub!

Finally, take a small amount of myrrh$_6$ oil (or some personal perfume if that's not available) in hand. Put a dab on various parts of your body while speaking a brief request for blessing to your image of the Great Spirit. Whatever you ask for during this time should reflect your ultimate goals as a Sacred Creation, and your immediate needs as a human being.

Here are some examples:
"Bless my eyes to see You in every portion of my life."
"Bless my feet that they can walk bravely on the path of beauty."
"Bless my hands to be strong but gentle towards my fellows"

"Bless my mouth to speak with kind sincerity."
"Bless my heart that it may freely give and receive love."
"Bless my mind for clear thought."
"Bless my ears that I may be a good listener for my
friends and family."

Don't worry about rushing out of the tub when you're
finished. Stay put and really let your anxiety wash away.
Watch as the tensions dispersed into the water move down the
drain. If it helps, try visualizing the water as almost muddy in
appearance, symbolizing the negative things you have left
there. Finally, write your impressions afterwards in your
journal. Repeat this exercise any time you feel the need.

Personal Diary — February 21, 1992

*"As a child, I prayed for my Mother, Father, sisters,
friends... everyone it seems but myself. Why? Did I think
God would only hear my prayers if they weren't about me?
Today is my birthday, and for a moment I plan to be the most
important person to the world... and I will begin by praying
for blessings for myself.*

*So much has happened in recent months, and there is a
lot of growing to digest. A little Divine sanction would be
welcome. Now, however, I return to God/dess not as a
frightened child, but a woman. As I approach the seat of
Knowledge and Wisdom, I am going to take a leap of faith,
believing that the universe has reason to heed one small,
sincere voice in the wilderness. That voice will be mine, and*

I will not stop until I am heard. Interestingly enough, the one who needs the most to heed these proclamations of worthiness is not God — the Spirit already knows my heart — but me."

Reflections

"At last they came to where reflection sits, a strange old woman, who had always one elbow on her knee, and her chin in her hand, and who steals light out of the past to shed it on the future."

— Olive Schreiner

There is nothing wrong with looking your best, as long as this "best" is what you want. For years I wore make up to work because I thought it was expected. I don't remember when, but one day I just stopped. No one but me even noticed the difference! The preconceived beliefs I had of the social demands in this setting proved wrong. I learned something very important from this experience. Now when I wear make up, it is for me, because I choose to, not to please others.

Sometimes we mistakenly blame a group, faction, or our culture for presenting repressive, superficial morals. The truth is, sometimes those ethics come from within. Be they remnants of past experience, something learned at the knee of a parent, or a partiality we developed ourselves, we need to recognize those weeds in our heart and pull them cleanly out.

Likenesses (Exercise 4)

When you have a few spare moments, stand in front of the bathroom mirror. Think about your negative contrivances. Are you quick to judge, intolerant of others, or too hung-up on details? Name each of the "weeds" in the garden of your life.

Next, take three deep breaths to center and calm your spirit. Name each contrivance one at a time, and visualize a face for that name. See it transforming over your own face in the mirror. Be prepared, this is not a pretty picture. Once the image is fully formed, denounce it. Tell this portion of yourself how you feel about that characteristic, command it to leave you and let the power of your sacred space begin its work. If desired, call upon the Great Spirit for aid.

As you talk to the portrait before you, and order its departure, your own face will slowly surface once more. You are always in control of your own fate, even the less desirable portions of your personality. Do not be afraid to seize the reigns of your life back! They are yours for the taking!

You may repeat this process with other aspects of self that need cleansing, but don't try to do it all in one day. You may find that the exercise has to be repeated for particularly stubborn traits. When this happens, don't be discouraged. We are not perfect, and some weeds are more deeply rooted than others. Till the soil, and just keep digging!

Cutting Away (Exercise 5)

The next time you shave, consider feelings or tendencies

in your life you want to "cut away." Focus your energy on those emotions or practices, voicing all the good reasons to purge them from your life. As the soap or shaving lotion gets collected on the blade, allow it to collect that negativity, then wash it neatly down the drain.

Repeat this exercise three times for each situation, while making other efforts on conventional levels to help those changes manifest. By the third repetition you should see some improvement in your demeanor. If no change comes, try repeating the activity seven times, the number of completion.

A gentle reminder here. Metaphysical techniques require that you match personal efforts on a mundane level with spiritual ones to be effective. Don't, for example, use this exercise to eliminate procrastination from your life, then immediately put off the first project that presents itself that day. The universe is not going to do all the work for you. If we are willing and desirous of helping our transformational journey, the universe will meet us half way.[7]

Flushing Out Negative Habits (Exercise 6)

One of the most marvelous modern inventions is indoor plumbing. For this activity, we are going to be putting it to a rather unique use. As in Exercise 5, focus on one negative habit, fixation or characteristic of yourself from which you really want to be freed. Write this on a small piece of paper and fold it three times.

Next, take a fire-proof container and place the paper within, sprinkling herbs traditionally used for purification on top. A good choice available in your own home is sage. Ignite the whole bundle, allowing the smoke to carry your desire to the Divine.

Last, but not least, flush the ashes down the toilet. Do not watch them as they leave — you have no need for those portions of self anymore. Just turn your back and walk away, vowing to start that very moment as a renewed being.

Personal Diary — March 1993

"I have discovered this unique portion of myself that I was afraid to face before. It is my dark cloud, my shadow and I have given her a name. Jokingly I call her Vivian, my evil step sister. In some ways, I envy this hidden side of myself -- she fearlessly expresses anger, frustration, cutting humor and even judgement without remorse. Such freedom! There is some part of her I could learn from, yet most of that aspect of self must remain quietly within. For goodness to mean something, it must have its shadow and Vivian is mine to overcome."

Gods and Goddesses of Beauty
"These things surely lie on the knees of the Gods."
— Homer

When it seems that all our attempts at self-transformation fail, sometimes it helps to see external assistance. Whether you call this eternal energy the Goddess, the Great Spirit, the Spark of the Big Bang, a Quark, Buddha, God, or by another name, the originating source is the same. And while the universe has its own sense of priorities that don't always mesh with our own, most often the call for aid will be answered. Down through the ages, various images of the Divine have been portrayed through the arts and written word. Each has some cultural flavor, and the unique characteristics they exhibit is awe inspiring. Among those likenesses, there should be at least one to which you feel drawn. Whether the country of origin tantalizes your curiosity, or because the portrait enkindles a beneficial emotional response, choose a Godd/ess to call when you need a little extra help.

Below are the names of several Gods and Goddesses from ancient and modern times, and all across the world. Each listing includes the Being's beneficial features. A few of these Beings are directly related to the ideal of Beauty such as Aphrodite and behaviors and qualities. As we call on these images, we likewise invoke the Spirit of those qualities, and welcome them into our lives.[8]

No matter what visage of God/ess you bring into your life, there is no need for pretense or fancy words. The Divine has known us at our best and worst (its part of the job description) and accepts you just as you are. Find a way to communicate to this Holy Power that is sincere, honest and open, and the results cannot help but be beneficial.

Adibuddha: Hindu god which personifies the perfected masculine attributes

Aengus: Irish god of love

Agloolik: Eskimo god of providence

Agni: Hindu benefactor of humankind and rain bringer

Ahsunnutli: American Indian god of balanced sexual energy

Ahura Mazda: Persian lord of knowledge and universal law

Aizen Myoo: Japanese god of compassion and empathy

Aker: Egyptian god of gateways and points of transition. Best called during times of drastic change, or when there seem to be barriers to opening doors in your life

Amathaon: Welsh god of magic

Amenowakahiko: Japanese god of courage

Amor: Roman god of love equivalent to the Greek Eros

Apollo: Greek god of creativity, the muse and arts

Asclepius: Greek god of healing

Ataksak: Eskimo god of joy

Baduh: Semitic god of communication

Baldur: Scandinavian god of wisdom

Bochica: Columbian god of arts and law

Bragi: Scandinavian god of sagacity and muse

Brihaspati: Hindu god of learning and education

Cilens: Etruscan guard of gates and portals (see notes on Aker)

Cronus: Phoenician god of time; good for people who need a stronger awareness for time management

Cupid: Greek god of romance

Dajdbug: Slavonic god of giving, the home and hearth

Dainichi: Japanese god of purity and wisdom

Damballah: Haitian benevolent father figure

Deuw Fidius: Roman god of hospitality

Dharma: Hindu god of faith

Diancecht: Irish god of healing

Ea: Chaldean god of discernment and magic

Ebisu: Japanese god of work

Enkidu: Sumerian friend to animals; excellent for improved insight into this facet of nature

Esmun: Phoenician god of well being

Fetket: Egyptian god of service

Fides: Roman god of honesty, especially in contractual bindings

Forseti: Scandinavian god of peace and justice

Fugen Bosatsu: Japanese god of intelligence and understanding

Fu Hsing: Chinese god of joy

Hashye Altye: Navajo communication god

Hatif: Arabic god of advise and warnings

Hephaestus: Greek god of craftsmen

Hermes: Greek god of messages, business and intelligence. Equivalent to the Roman Mercury

Horus: Egyptian god whose eyes of the sun and moon lend perspective

Hotei: Japanese god of mirth

Itzamna: Mayan god who fathered mankind

Janus: Roman god of cycles (to encourage or break)

Kamu-nahobi: Japanese god who corrects inequity and wrong doing

Kannon Bosatu: Japanese god of sympathy

Khephra: Egyptian god of self creation; excellent choice for personal transformative work

K'uei-hsing: Chinese god of scrutiny; good choice if alertness to details is needed

Lono: Polynesian god of fruitfulness

Min: Egyptian god of sexuality

Misharu: Assyro-Babylonian god of uniformity, continuity. Helps move situations back into an even keel

Morpheus: Greek god of dreams and vision

Neter: Egyptian ultimate male divinity

Odin: Scandinavian god of shrewdness

Omacatl: Aztec god of merrymaking

Prometheus: Greek god of foresight

Savitar: Hindu god of action and motion

Silenus: Greek servant to Dionysus who always had perceptive advice

Sin: Chaldean god of time

Tengu: Japanese playful spirits to awaken the child within

Tien-kuan: Chinese god of blessings

Tvashtar: Hindu god of motivation and zeal, perfect for

procrastinators

Urcaguay: Incan god of hidden treasures, usually pertains to financial matters but can indirectly be focused towards spiritual gifts

Vanir: Scandinavian gods of protection

Visvakarma: Hindu god of means & methods; effective for right-brain thinking

Xochipilli: Aztec god of fertility, marriage, and youthful aspirations

Yang: Chinese active male principle

Yarilo: Slavonic god of ardor

Yazatas: Persian gods of morality

Goddesses:

Adishakti: Hindu Goddess of feminine energy

Aeons: Gnostic embodiment of power, strength and origins

Aima: Hebrew Goddess of fertility & productivity

Alaisiagae: Roman Goddess of service who teaches us giving

Aleitheia: Gnostic Goddess of truth, especially with ourselves

Amaterasu: Japanese Goddess of illumination; sun energy

Anagke: Greek Goddess of necessity and fate

Angerona: Roman Goddess of silence, a valuable teacher

Aphrodite: Greek Goddess of sexual love

Aramati: Hindu Goddess of devotion (individual or circumstantial)

Artemis: Greek Lunar Goddess who encourages psychic flow

Asgaya Gigagei: American Indian God/dess who is bisexual; good choice to help balance yin-yang energies

Asteraea: Greek Goddess of fairness and virtue

Atergatis: Syrian Goddess of new beginnings; an excellent choice for exercise 1 in chapter 2 (The Pledge)

Athena: Powerful Greek Goddess who embodied leadership, intelligence and a love of the arts

Baalat: Phoenician paramount icon of "the Lady"₉

Belit-ilanit: Chaldean Goddess of peaceful intentions and eros

Benten: Japanese Goddess of eloquence, serendipity and prosperity

Bharati: Hindu Goddess of speech and effective communications

Binah: Hebrew Goddess of manifestation and understanding

Cabiro: Phoenician Goddess of deep mysteries and a powerful early type of the ultimate feminine aspect

Cerridwin: Welsh Goddess of inspiration and creativity

Concordia: Roman Goddess of harmony, especially in groups.

Dahud: Breton Goddess of sexual freedom. An effective option for people working on their sense of passion and sensuality

Deu: Indian Goddess who is the ultimate motherly, creative love

Dorje-Naljorma: Tibetan Goddess of feminine occult potency. Good choice for any womens' mystery rites

Graces, The: Greek muses who personifies song, dance and joy

Epinoia: Gnostic Goddess who teaches the power of thought and creativity

Fides: Roman Goddess of faithfulness and trust

Filia Vocis: Hebrew Goddess of Divine vision

Freya: Teutonic beloved Goddess of the moon, marriage and resourcefulness

Habondia: Medieval Goddess of witches whose name implies abundance

Harmonia: Greek Goddess of accord, especially in matters of the heart

Hathor: Egyptian Goddess who personify the purest feminine qualities

Hebe: Greek Goddess of youthfulness (this can also apply to youthful ideas or energy)

Hecate: Greek Goddess of crone wisdom, excellent matron to older men and women seeking after ancient Mysteries

Ida: Hindu Goddess of many positive attributes including speech, foresight, reverence and the learning of occult ideology

Ibaluris: Hittite Goddess of Divine missives

Isis: Egyptian Goddess who is the most complete figure of the feminine divine aspect ever seen in history

Ixalvoh: Mayan Goddess of weaving who can help us reinforce and guide the fibers of our Sacred Self

Kaikilani: Polynesian Goddess of beauty

Kamrusepas: Hittite Goddess of well-being and magic

Karakarook: Australian Goddess who defends women in need

Kebehut: Egyptian Goddess of refreshment, newness

Khamden: Hindu Goddess of desire and wishes

Kichijo-Ten: Japanese Goddess of beauty and luck

Kikimora: Slavonic Goddess of the home and domestic arts

Korraval: Hindu Goddess of success and victory

Kukun-Hime: Japanese Goddess of negotiation

K'un: Chinese Goddess of nourishment & preservation

Lakshimi: Hindu Goddess of beauty, luck and prosperity$_{10}$

Lasya: Tibetan Goddess of complete loveliness

Liban: Irish Goddess of pleasure

Ma$_{11}$: Lydian fertility Goddess

Manasa: Hindu Goddess who fought the patriarchy and chauvinism

Maya: Hindu creator Goddess, giver of life, knowledge and magic

Medhbh: Irish Goddess of warrior energy

Meni: Chaldean Goddess of adoration and destiny

Minerva: Roman protective Goddess for business and education

Mnemosyne: Greek Goddess of memory and recollection

Mylitta: Assyro-Babylonian Goddess of love, attractiveness, and fundicity

Namagin: Hindu Goddess of inspiration, foresight and education

Neith: Egyptian Goddess who is the eternal feminine principal

Nerthus: Teutonic Goddess of harmony and productivity

Nike: Greek Goddess of achievement, mastery and success

Ninkarrak: Chaldean Goddess who puts right all misfortune

Nisaba: Chaldean Goddess of building, may be called upon for construction of the Sacred Self

Ops: Roman Goddess of sewing and reaping to help us harvest our labors

Parvati: Hindu Goddess of power, grace and brilliance

Prajna-Paramita: Eastern Asian Goddess who personifies ultimate sagacity

Rati: Hindu Goddess of pleasure and passion

Sefkhet-seshat: Egyptian Goddess of record keeping

Shala: Sumerian Goddess of compassion and empathy

Shekinah: Hebrew personification of divine illumination

Sodas: Hindu Goddess of flawlessness and excellence

Sophia: Gnostic representation of creative sexual energy

Tashmit: Chaldean Goddess of listening and answered prayers

Til Bu Ma: Tibetan Goddess of strict equity

Tui: Chinese visage of gentleness

Ushas: Hindu Goddess of dawn, beginnings, joy, blessings and beauty

Xochiquetzal: Aztec Goddess of love, marriage and happiness

Yachimato Hime: Japanese Goddess of many roads (choices)

Yeshe Khadoma: Tibetan Goddess of mystical fulfillment

Yesod: Hebrew bi-sexual attribute of foundations, strength and manifestation

Finding Divinity Within (Exercise 7)

For this activity, locate a physical image that reflects all the qualities you envision in the Divine. Additionally, gather one white candle, one candle of your favorite color and take both to the bathroom mirror.

Study the chosen image carefully until you can see it clearly in your mind's eye. Next, light the white candle and focus your attention on it. Breath slowly and evenly until you feel calm. Notice how the glow of the candle fills the room.

Feel its warmth touching you. Continue to extend your senses as you close your eyes.

Now, visualize that same candle burning within the center of your being. It is vibrant and alive. Around the flame of the candle see the face of the Divine image studied earlier slowly forming. Watch as it radiates with power, wisdom and assurance. Try and keep this vision firmly in mind.

Now, open your eyes long enough to light the second candle from the flame of the first. This candle represents your spirit being ignited by Divine energy. Leave the candles together, and close your eyes once more.

Still envision the first candle forming the face of the Divine, but now also see the other nearby with your own image surrounding it. The two lights are bright, almost blinding in their beauty, but neither overcomes the other. Slowly imagine the two candles becoming one, with the image of the God/dess and your own likewise merging, then open your eyes.

Look immediately into the mirror and see the perfect picture of Spirit and individual in harmony. In the window of your soul, look to the Divine light that now shines outward. Accept that bit of God-Self within, and welcome it as a cherished friend. Know that this exercise is not necessary for Spirit to abide in your heart. It is already there, working with you every day; you are Divine!

The Shower of Blessings (Exercise 8)

This activity requires nothing more than a little time and

a good imagination. The next time you take a shower, think of the water as luminous drops of sparkling energy. Sometimes it helps to visualize the shower head as your image of the God/dess (chosen in Exercise 7), from whom all blessings flow.

As the energy pellets slide over your skin, allow them to absorb all sickness, all weariness, all tension, then move easily down the drain. Once you feel completely relaxed, change the color of your energy-shower to one that revitalizes you. For example, fiery people might find red energizes them, while earth-centered personalities find power in green shades.

This time, as the drops hit your body, allow them to release power with each splash. See this energy appearing like glitter that, at first, surrounds you in a cloud. Then, the cloud moves inward and gets absorbed through your pores, effectively refilling the well of self. Continue with this visualization until you feel thoroughly refreshed. Afterwards, have a soothing cup of tea while making notes in your journal.

Personal Diary — October 1988

"A friend told me this wonderful story today, about how at the beginning of time God shattered into millions of tiny mirror-like pieces, each one lodging in a soul. This way we would never really be separate from that Creator Spirit, but could always look within to find reflections of the best we can be.

It amazed me that such a simple tale could be so wise. With one fable, I found I understood my own feelings about the God/dess better. All the Gods of antiquity are facets of one great crystal, each one reflecting different aspects of human nature. In one of those visages, each person can find something to relate to; to desire — so that eventually our spiritual thirst leads us home to the temple of our own hearts."

Notes

1. Some people may feel that their bedroom is a more appropriate spot than the bath depending on where they spend the most time looking in a mirror and taking care of the physical nature. If so, adapt these ideas to that room wherever feasible. In this case you might look to symbolic patterns in pillow cases, sheets, quilts and mirror frames instead of the bath-related items discussed.

2. Ancient folk traditions often used the symbolism of the moon in preparing foods or medicines. Bread and beer might be brewed during a waxing moon to insure they rose properly, while prescriptions for diseases were prepared when the moon waned so sickness would shrink.

3. As far back in human history as Ancient Egypt and probably beyond, colors carried mystical portent especially for the folk healer who depended on "sympathy" for many cures. Here, yellow plant parts were used to cure jaundice while red parts were for blood problems.

   Scents have made a come-back recently through aromatherapy, but the early perfumers were certainly aware of their power to effect the human state. Most ascribed floral or herbal aromas are closely connected with their magical attributes given by alchemists, mages and Cunning folk throughout the ages.

potent for divination as well as protection.

5. Even people who are afraid of water are usually quite at ease in a tub. If your fears are too strong, apply this section to a shower or warm foot soak instead.

6. Oil of Myrrh was one of the original anointing oils for the priests of the Hebrew temples, making it very appropriate in a setting where you are your own Priest/ess.

7. The only time this doesn't happen is when a particular lesson must be learned alone. There are some sojourns in life that, in order to have lasting meaning, must be solitary. The universe is not cruel, but it is practical, responding to both immediate needs and the highest good.

8. Divine images should always be approached with appropriate respect and forethought. Take time to learn about the spirit to whom you're calling so that you can honor them suitably in your sacred space. For two excellent resources on the Gods and Goddesses of the world, try Janet & Stewart Farrar's *The Witches God*, and *The Witches Goddess*. For prices and ordering information contact Phoenix Publishing, Portal Way, Box 10, Custer WA 98240.

9. Even as the Catholic church sometimes refers to Mary as "our Lady," the Goddess in earlier times was known by this simple title. In contemporary magical traditions, May Day is sometimes called Lady Day and is a celebration of the feminine aspect of the Divine.

   As a note of interest, The term lady comes from the

Anglo Saxon meaning loaf giver (or provider) and was a term of great honor.

10. In reading this list, it is impossible not to notice that many of the Goddesses who are strongly associated with beauty are also identified with good fortune, as if this attribute itself was "lucky."

11. The term "MA" as being part of the name for a Goddess is very common throughout the world. The God/dess is the symbol of universal motherhood and the creative spark. Notably, "ma" is the first sound a baby usually makes when suckling.

Five:
Personal Care

"The ideal beauty is, therefore, true natural beauty, and that to which all mankind will still advance with advancing knowledge and civilization."

— Arnold Cooley

"Health must be there, or beauty cannot be"

— Anon.

The Sacred Space of home has been defined, and the beings within are likewise holy. But even those among us considered saintly in demeanor often have difficulty reaching out and asking for help. For that matter, they find it troublesome to expend the same energy on themselves as they do in caring for others. You probably know at least one person like this — someone who should wear a pin that says "stop me before I volunteer again." Perhaps that someone is you.

Even if you aren't quite that zealous, I can almost guarantee that you hesitate to indulge yourself periodically. Things like sleeping in, taking a walk alone, or buying yourself a treat may seem like minor considerations, but in the quest for wholeness you should not view them as insignificant. Many minute things in our daily routine effect our welfare. Not the least of these is the way we attend our physical nature.

The body can not be neglected without consequence. If

you consider the word disease as a compound (dis-ease), you can see that even a subtle disregard for our health may prove detrimental to our physical and spiritual being. Thus, the goal of this chapter is to refocus your awareness on the way you care for yourself.

A Healthful Diet:

"One should eat to live, not live to eat"
— Benjamin Franklin

Before you are tempted to skip this section altogether, I absolutely promise that it is not a lecture on the evils of salt, junk food or cholesterol. I happen to love pizza, soda and Twinkies, and have no intention of removing such joys from my diet or yours. Instead, consider this an opportunity to encourage a little more thoughtfulness in your cooking and eating habits.

We are living in a very hectic world where all of us, at one time or another, skip meals or eat whatever is expedient. If this continues regularly for a few weeks, we become too sick or weary to do anything productive. When the physical nature gets ignored, sickness or exhaustion is our body's cry for attention.

I find myself in that situation more often than I might like to admit, so this section is written as a gentle nudge to myself too. The body is the instrument of our soul's learning in this world. If it is not well, the spirit can not function at its best. It is the simple law of "as without, so within," working on a very intimate level.

Rather than repeating the nutritional guides that you've heard since your youth, my main recommendation is this: eat balanced meals whenever you can. Plan ahead by freezing hearty leftovers for quick meals. If you have a "craving" for an unusual food item (not chocolate), it may be your body's way of expressing what it needs. Listen to that voice.

If you do get busy and eat "instant" everything, try to take a little extra time on calmer days to prepare solid meals. Pay particular attention to include all the "building blocks" for good health. If this is not viable, ask your pharmacist to recommend a daily supplement.

Please don't forget to rest! All work and no play not only makes "Jack a dull boy," but also subjects "Jack" to any number of illnesses that could have been avoided by a decent nights sleep. Everything you want to accomplish in your goal of achieving the Sacred Self will show far better results when your body is rested and nourished.

With just a little forethought, a healthy diet can be attained without tremendous amounts of preparation. If you can't have breakfast because you overslept, consider a glass of fruit juice for revitalization. Some fast-food restaurants offer foods made with less oil and fat, which can take the place of a home-made lunch. Then there's the frozen food industry offering low-fat, low cholesterol menus, as an alternative fast and hearty dinner.

Thankfully, the commercial world now recognizes that people's schedules and the desire to stay healthy don't always work agreeably together. For the spiritual seeker this realization is doubly important. Finding innovative combinations of New Age and material approaches for maintaining the body improves every part of our reality.

One such innovation may already exist in your own back yard! Nature provided humankind with the most wonderful pantry to select from, stuffed full with nutritional value. Here, a wealth of options for cooking and personal enrichment present themselves unwittingly disguised as roots, leaves, flowers, trees and pantry herbs. Below are just a few examples of some unique substitutions that are fairly available in diverse climates. These options will help you in your efforts to eat healthier, and a little more creatively!

Nuts: Replace with asparagus, barley, hyssop, prickly pear, or water lily seeds which are roasted.

Coffee: Replace with chicory or dandelion root, juniper berry, sunflower, aspen or barley seeds, all of which should be roasted and ground.

Soups: Add sorrel, angelica and watercress leaf, nettle root and sunflower heads boiled.

Flour: Try alfalfa stems, beech and hickory nuts, cattail and red clover blossoms, burdock root, horsetail stems, leek bulbs, maize kernels and white oak acorns all dried and ground fine.

Gum: Roots of dandelion, chicory, licorice and plantain

Oil: Sunflower seed or wintergreen leaf crushed and boiled.

In addition to this list, many of the spices, vegetables, and fruits that we enjoy regularly are a secret warehouse for nutrients. Flowers also have many vitamins (be sure they are edible, however). If you find that your diet is lacking in certain essentials, take a look at the following list and see what you can eat to bring balance back to your body. Also, please check with your personal physician. Vitamin deficiencies can be warning signs to other, more serious problems.

Vitamin A: Warning signs - poor appetite and digestion, brittle hair or nails, gum infections. Foods recommended: chicken or turkey sandwich on whole wheat bread. Oatmeal with raisins. Apple yogurt. Fruit salad with cantaloupe, grapes, banana and pineapple. Fish with asparagus, carrots or peas on the side.

Vitamin B complex: Warning signs: mood swings, skin disorders, weariness sleep disorders, anemia, nervousness, dizziness. Foods recommended: Whole grain cereal with strawberries. Brewers yeast sprinkled on plain popcorn. Banana yogurt. Eggnog with raspberries. Green peppers and carrots with blue cheese dressing. Fish or corn chowders. Creamed turkey with broccoli.

Vitamin C: Warning signs: frequent colds and flu, slow healing of cuts or breaks, easy bruising, nose bleeds. Foods recommended: Bran flakes with yogurt instead of milk, chicken with oranges, stuffed haddock, dandelion salad, tofu dishes, lots of citrus fruit, rosehip tea.

Vitamin D: Warning signs: diarrhea, rapid changes in weight, decreased energy, restless or jittery nature, bad tooth decay. Foods recommended: raisin bran with skim milk and bananas. Tuna melts.

Vitamin E: Warning signs - fertility problems, kidney or liver infections, gas and upset stomach. Foods recommended: Corn and banana bread, strawberry-orange juice, spinach pies, glazed carrots with parsley, strawberry-apple pie (made with honey instead of sugar).

Vitamin K: Warning signs: easy bleeding, miscarriage, prolonged diarrhea. Foods recommended: banana oatmeal cookies, cornmeal raisin bread, peaches and strawberries in cream, creamed chicken with asparagus or broccoli, tomatoes.

Iron: Warning signs: sluggish energy, many colds, poor circulation, anemia, brittle nails. Foods recommended: oatmeal raisin cookies, broiled fish, pumpkin pie, stuffed mushrooms with cheese, lentil soup.

Personal Diary — August 1987

"When I was carrying Karl, all I seemed to crave was radishes, pickles, onions and other vegetables. I vividly remember the pleasure found in these foods; one that I have yet to totally discover again.

Everyone laughed at me, thinking as most people that cravings are just a psychological state. Now that Karl is older, they aren't laughing any more! Most children stick up their noses at such things, but Karl would rather have veggies than meat or candy... chives, broccoli and radishes fresh from the garden being favorites. It's odd that it took me two years to consciously realize what my body understood all along; I wasn't feeding only my own hunger but meeting certain dietary needs of that life within me."

Food Monitoring (Exercise 1)

For one week, keep a pad and paper with you, marking down everything you eat including cups of coffee, candy bars, munchies, and gum. Also make notes about how you feel each day upon rising, around lunch time, at dinner, and before bed. At the end of the week, take a look at what you have consumed. Next to the less nutritional items, make a list of healthier alternatives. Granola bars, carrot or celery sticks, and dried fruits can substitute for candy and other snack items, for example.

The next step is to make a menu that you can feasibly stick to and afford for one whole week. If possible, include three balanced meals a day, and nutritive snacks. Commit yourself to adhere to this menu as closely as possible (no snitching!) so you can adequately gauge success or failure when the activity is completed. As before, make note of how you feel throughout the day. Consider how alert you are both physically and spiritually.

It is likely that none of us will be able to stick to perfect diets throughout our lives. Even so, this activity makes you more intimately aware of the value of eating well, and your normal eating habits. Use this exercise the week before a special occasion so you can look and feel your best.

Finally, one small convention regarding food often gets overlooked today — that of praying at mealtime. Prayer, or a moment of meditation, is a way to change our attitude and ask the Greater Powers that only the best of our food be accepted by the body. This is also a moment wherein families and friends can gather quietly, and reaffirm their unity.

Exercise
"Health is the vital principle of bliss, and exercise of health"
— **James Thomson**

Rather like brushing your teeth as a child, daily exercise is a marvelous habit to get into, but one not so easily maintained when you get busy. So, the trick in any good exercise program is to find one that meshes with your schedule. Don't commit yourself to jogging every morning if you're not a morning person, or if early meetings are common in your agenda. Instead, try to find safe, effective activities that you can add easily to your day.

Take the dog for an extra long walk daily, or go for an evening swim at the YMCA. Follow your chosen routine as regularly as other daily habits. For individuals with a history of physical problems, please consult with your physician first before embarking on any exercise program. If they say "no" to your idea, they will likely have other safe suggestions.

Walk the Walk (Exercise 2)

One of the safest, and best, exercises is walking. Almost every Doctor will gladly recommend a hearty stroll after meals or before bed time to improve digestion and sleep. For this activity we will take the idea of walking one step further by adding a visualization for improved self images.

No matter when you choose to walk, try to move toward a light source. A street lamp, the moon, the sun, or a lighted window across the way are all good examples. Wear a good, supportive pair of shoes, and take the time to breath deeply. Feel how the fresh air revitalizes you.

While you walk, think of the grass or pavement beneath your feet as your life's path. When you look at your feet, you can't seem to tell where you're going. When you focus all your attention on the light, however, the path is clear.

Walk slowly and purposefully now, naming each step after part of your spiritual quest. Step one might be "the beginning," two is "growth," three "initiation," four "insight," five "compassion," and so on. Each step is one positive attribute you are bringing closer, even as you get closer to the source of illumination, symbolic of the Divine spark.

After naming all the characteristics you can think of, continue looking toward the light. Think about some of situations over the last week that left you out of balance. Move yourself to the point of an observer in that scenario, and allow the light to guide your vision. Also allow it to shine within your heart, and cast away any shadows hiding there.

Once you reach the lighted area, relax a bit before returning home. When you turn to walk back, know that the light is always there even though you can't see it now. Tuck a bit of that assurance in your pocket for tomorrow, and let it shine through your day.

Personal Diary — May 1993

"It's nice to take a daily walk. Besides getting me away from the office, I find I really look forward to it now. At first, my lazy bones were content to stay and sit at my desk. But once the routine was established it became a time to shop, people watch, contemplate, or go get a good book from the library. Suddenly I find I'm disappointed when it rains -- then again, maybe I should keep boots and an umbrella handy!"

Clothing

*"Sorrow hath no sympathy with fashion, and outward grace
decays when inward joy hath perish'd."*

— E.H. Burrington

There has always been some disparagement between what culture regarded as beautiful and necessary, and what religion dictated as appropriate. On one hand the individual fights for expression. On the other hand, you have an organization trying to prescribe that expression.

Yet, despite this social tug of war, even the Church was not without some decorative raiment to set its priestly cast apart. Ancient Hebrew clerics wore bells around their skirts. The high priest had a special breastplate with twelve semi-precious stones inlaid, representing the tribes of Israel. Druidical leaders sometimes wore special robes and jewelry to celebrate festivals like Eisteddfod, an ancient bardic competition. Even today the robes of the Catholic hierarchy display rich, gold and white splendor.[1]

Now that we have begun to accept the role of our own High Priest/ess in rebuilding sacred beauty within, there is nothing wrong with marking the new position in our lives accordingly. It is the form and manner of identification that is really the heart of the question here. How do we apply the old notion of "clothes make the man" in a spiritually significant and constructive manner?

Every item we wear reflects our personality in some way. The color, line, texture and how all the pieces work together reveals a little about who we are, and how we think, to those around us. In different settings, these "costumes" change. Yet, certain subtle idiosyncrasies remain the same. These small touches are an expression of your individuality to the world. With a little ingenuity, you can also use such garnishes to help support the foundations of your Sacred Self. One individual might wear a fresh flower every day in their hair or lapel to express their love of nature. Another might add a silk scarf to encourage more flowing energy in their daily existence. Another yet, makes sure they don at least one blue item each day for a month so that the power of tranquility moves into their lives. Each person in these three illustrations has found a way to declare their individuality, and blend that identity with their spiritual goals and needs.

This is a tremendously potent combination for personal transformation. Instead of compartmentalizing the mundane from the esoteric, this technique works with the *whole* person. Yet it does so with a minimum of pomp, so you can maintain seemly costumes for whatever settings life hands you.

Symbolic Clothing (Exercise 3)

Below is a list of common attire and possible associations for spiritual goals. To this list, add at least ten specific items from your own wardrobe and their meanings as you perceive them. Consider their color, their traditional environment, when they were purchased (or by whom), and what memories they engender. Adopt at least one or two of these as embellishments into your daily wardrobe, thereby proclaiming your sacred self to the world.

Item	Possible Meanings
Necktie	Frugality, prudence, restraint
Tie Tack or Pins	Penetration, staying-power, foundation
Socks	Warmth, friendship (they come in pairs) health
Handkerchief	Virtue, honor, neatness
Jeans	Comfort, leisure, adventure
Suit	Restrictions, constraints, formality
Sneakers	Quiet, caution, support, movement
Dress shoes	Respect, decorum, civility
Shorts	Pleasure, leisure, activity
Rain Coat	Protection, shelter
Underwear	Motherly advise, sensuality
White T-Shirt	Purification, safety, cleanliness

Dress Up (Exercise 4)

On your next day off try something fun and liberating. When you get up, make the entire day thematic starting with your clothing. As with Exercise 3, consider all your wearable items as having potential to help with personal change. Find a mix-n-match group that vibrantly portrays your goal. If you are having a whole morning dedicated to physical exercise, for example, choose bright, sunny colored sweats or leotards for improved energy. Don't worry if what you pick out wouldn't suit a fashion expert; you're going to please *yourself* today.

Besides the clothing, keep everything throughout that day along the same composition. For the above example, drink fresh juices, eat only vegetables, fruits and grains, enjoy a sauna, go swimming, and take a long walk. Possibly team up with a friend who has similar goals. Encourage each other, and enjoy the company.

Jewelry

"How many a thing which we cast to the ground, when others pick it up, it becomes a gem"

— George Merideth

The New Age market place is filled to over flowing with shiny objects made by talented crafts people. Semi-precious metals and stones sit scattered across display cases to tempt the buyer's eye. What is it about these sparkling trinkets that so enamors us?

The lore of precious gems and metals is as long and lustrous as the items themselves. From the first moment that light danced off a slightly polished surface, superstitions started to grow like facets around jewels. Be it carrying a stone that signifies your birth month for luck, or wearing copper to encourage health, jewelry is another functional tool to help generate personal change.

How do you choose what to wear? Much the same way you sorted your wardrobe earlier this chapter. A list of common stones and metals is provided below along with their associations. Bear in mind, however, that if a stone carries different meaning for you, use that correlation instead. These items are seen all day long, thereby providing our subconscious mind with a gentle "nudge" toward a specific energy matrix.

This continual silent suggestion builds synchronous vibrations$_2$ around us that coincide with our goals. To put this idea into a functional vignette, let's say you're struggling with a lack of forbearance. Instead of positing a sign at your work station that says "FORTITUDE," you might wear a piece of diamond jewelry regularly for a while. Being the sturdiest gem known, the diamond represents the characteristics of perseverance and strength in the quest for Sacredness.[3]

Stone/Metal	Common Associations
Silver	Feminine attributes, lunar energy, unconscious mind, intuitive nature healing, creativity, fertility
Gold	Masculine attributes, solar energy, conscious mind, strength, intelligence, leadership, action, vigor
Copper	Conduction, movement, well-being
Iron	Foundations, grounding
Tin	Serendipity, good fortune
Amber	Captured energy, alertness, endings[4]
Amethyst	Sobriety, dignity, temperance administration, resolutions
Beryl	Kinship, agile mental energy
Carnelian	Protection, wishes, composure
Coral	Physical energy, sagacity, water qualities
Gypsum	Clarity, safety and good luck
Hematite	Victory, attainment, success
Jade	Love, fruitfulness, well-being
Loadstone	Attraction, charm
Moonstone	Spiritual insight, lunar energy
Turquoise	Timeliness, safety, healing

Making a Medicine Bag (Exercise 5)

For this activity you will need about 18 inches of leather thong, two nine-inch pieces of sturdy string, two 5 x 5 squares of cloth (your choice, preferably a natural material), and a collection of small stones, shells and other natural objects that have special meaning to you.

Take the squares of cloth and sew them by hand on three sides. Leave about 3/4" at the top open on both sides so you can make a channel for the drawstring & thong. Next, stitch a path for the thong, taking care to finish off any rough edges by doubling under the fabric. Turn the pouch right side out so the seam is inside. Attach the thong to a safety pin and draw it through the channel. Finally, lace through the two 9" pieces going opposite directions for draw strings.

When you've finished with the pouch, take out the treasures you have gathered. Name each according to what they represent, then place them within. Periodically wear the bag as a necklace. Carry a little bit of nature's bounty with you to sensitively stimulate the transformations desired.

Tatoos:

Most who subject themselves to the tattooer's needle know little of the rich history of this art. In it's earliest forms, tatoos were not always permanent, but a temporary means of illustrating something specific. The Celts wore wode to scare the enemy during battle. Certain tribal cultures indicated an individual's undertaking of a sacred quest with special body paints and dyes.

Later, tatoos marked the members of a tribe similarly to show their unity. They provided a kind of portable history, where any significant moment in an individual's life was etched upon them for the world to see.

Today tattooing has the ambiance of an artform, and is still a means for personal expression. If you don't like the idea of a permanent tatoo, temporary body paints are an alternative. Either approach offers a way to set yourself apart. Use an inspirational symbol whose meaning is reinforced each time you, or others, look upon it.

Symbolic Body Painting (Exercise 6)

For this activity you will need a paint brush and some water soluble body paints. Generally, this exercise is most productive for expelling negative thought patterns and bad habits.

Start by making a list of the things that you are consciously striving to change. Next, give each habit or tendency a symbolic form. Quick anger might be visually emblemized by a lightning bolt, for example. Paint the images nearest the part of your body that is most directly influencing them. Using the aforementioned example, the lightning bolt might get drawn near your temple.

When you are finished, look closely at yourself in a mirror. Are these things a true representation of the Divinity within? If not, take a shower and wash them neatly down the drain. Make a promise to yourself and the Divine to continue your daily efforts for improvement.

Repeat this activity as often as you want to intensify the effect. It is not necessarily a fast cure-all. Releasing life-long conventions can take a while. Just be patient and consistent, knowing an honest desire for change is a tremendous ally for attaining holiness within and without.

Hair Styles:

"And beauty draws us with a single hair"
— **Alexander Pope**

To our youth, "wild" hairstyles are one way to buck the establishment and make a public statement about their feelings. They are not the first to discover this avenue for expression, however. The hippies made long tresses into part of the revolution of the 1960's, including a musical entitled simply "Hair."

Almost everyone knows the story of Samson whose strength was in his hair. In the Hebrew culture, a Jewess' crowning glory was her hair. In fact, some Eastern lands so revered beautiful, silky locks that hair became a type of currency, cut and traded for food and other necessities.

During the Victorian era, small snippets of hair found their way into mementos between lovers and dear friends. Braided hair is sometimes used in bonding rites for parents and children, or between newlyweds even today. In some neo-pagan traditions hair may become part of a personal incense, medicine pouch or potion. In all cases, hair lends potency to the effort because it is so intimate.

So, our feelings about hair, no matter how silly they might initially seem, have very deep roots (excuse the pun). Exploring this a little further, a change in hair style or coloration could illustrate personal shifts in demeanor. Many monastic orders, for example, shave or cut their hair upon taking their life vows to show their separation from worldly ways. Rostafarians, conversely, grow long thick locks so that when God returns, he can take them to heaven by the strands. In both cases, the way the hair is worn (or not) indicates a specific spiritual conviction important to that individuals' chosen Path.

Color Me Lovely (Exercise 7)

Just as with clothing, a different hair style can make us feel different even if the alteration is only temporary. Have you always wanted to be a blond? Try a temporary dye and see if it changes your perspective. Want to see what it would be like with short hair? Instead of drastic cutting, how about buying or borrowing a wig for a week?

The change here has little to do with outward appearance. Instead it focuses on the way you respond to your transformed image. Any modifications you can make that improve your self image are good as long as they don't become a crutch. Sacred beauty relies on the internal loveliness of the soul, not what the concrete externals.

Cologne And Perfume
"Pomades & perfume rejoice the heart."
— **Proverbs 27:9**

In the last chapter I spoke briefly about aromatherapy. The ideas behind this technique are actually very old. Several of the most renowned herbalists in history spoke of the benefits of aromas. When they weren't singing a herb's praises, both commoners and monarch's alike were employing scents to beautify, tempt, and allure.

Cleopatra placed hundreds of rose petals on her floor before Mark Anthony's visits to secure his love. Pliney the Elder, John Gerald, and other noted herbalists spoke of lily as comforting the heart, motherwort as a cure for melancholy, and the scent of rosemary as improving awareness.

Moving these time-honored concepts into our lives is not difficult. Most people react strongly to specific fragrances. Just consider the stomach-grumbling that fresh baked bread inspires, for example.

One of the easiest ways to use aromatherapy for self transformation is through perfumes, colognes and potpourri. Originally, the word perfume meant "through smoke," indicating that incense was really the first universal aromatic. Later, as the Arabic world refined the art of the perfumer, some of the most highly valued scents traveled the trade routes to please the most discriminating of noses. With merchants and explorers, the lore of fragrances and their marvelous powers likewise traveled throughout Europe and eventually to the New World.

Make your own Scent (Exercise 8)

Think about your favorite natural fragrances and how they make you feel. Does pine refresh you? Does rose inspire romantic thoughts? Find one, two or three base materials that coincide with the goals of your Sacred Path. Dried culinary spices work very well, as do many other parts of trees, shrubs, and roots. However, the general rule of "the fresher the better" definitely applies.

The chosen aromas should mix nicely together without becoming overpowering. Additionally, flower petals should be fresh, free of any leaves or debris, and picked before the sun strikes them. Take a moment to bless your chosen ingredients in a manner suitable to your faith.

Warm a cup of almond or olive oil over a low flame in a

non-aluminum pot. Add your herbs to the oil slowly. If you have a tea ball or bit of cheese cloth, wrap the herbs within so you won't have to strain the oil later. Flower petals should set until their color is gone and they appear translucent. You need about one cup of petals to each cup of oil. Other herbs, especially dried ones, require smaller amounts. With pungent herbs like cinnamon, as little as a half teaspoon can produce pleasing results. Finding just the right balance may take a little bit of experimentation, but the effort is well worth it.

Finally, house your personal scent in a decorative, air-tight bottle. Wear it when performing self blessings, when going somewhere special or any time you want to reinforce self-importance. Use it to anoint personal items of deep emotional values, put some in the ritual bath (see chapter 2) or on small sachets for your drawers.

As you enjoy the aroma, it will gently empower your spiritual aspirations and inspire positive actions to meet those goals. Here are some sample combinations that I find both enjoyable and metaphysically beneficial:

For Blessing/Inspiration
1 Tsp. Lavender flowers
1 Tsp. Rosemary dried
1/2 orange rind diced
1/2" sliver of sandalwood
1 Tsp. geranium petals

Refreshed Perspectives
1 Tsp. Anise
1 Tsp. Thyme
1/2 lemon rind diced
dash Marjoram
1 Tsp. Angelica

Breaking Bad Habits
1 Tsp. Wintergreen
2-3 whole Cloves
1 Tsp. Lilac petals

Cleansing/Purification
1 Tbs. pine needles
1/2 Tsp. Frankincense
1/2 Tsp. Myrrh

3 Elder leaves   1/2" piece Cedar wood
3 Bay leaves   1/2 Tsp. Mint

Compassion/Empathy

1/2 Tsp. Basil
1 Tsp. Cyclamen
1/2 Tsp. Lemon juice
2 Bay leaves
2 Celery leaves

Spiritual Vision

1/2 stick Cinnamon
1/2 tsp. dried Lemonbalm
1 Tsp. dried Rose petals
3 strands Saffron
1/2 Tsp. Thyme

Sacred Beauty

3 whole violet flowers or morning glories
1 Tsp. catnip
1/2 Tsp. ginseng
1 cup of dew gathered on May Day
3 Daisy's (petals only)
2 roses (1 pink, one white - petals only)
1 apple (peel only)

To give you an idea of how these recipes were derived, let's look at this last one specifically. Violet aids supernatural understanding. So, three violet flowers symbolically strengthen spirituality; three being the number of body-mind and soul. The next three ingredients have a connection with beauty, may dew also being purported to remove freckles! Pink and white roses encourage friendship and peace within the self (color emblems) and apple is for overall well-being (note the old saying "an apple a day, keeps the doctor away)."

If you have allergies, or are particularly sensitive to skin preparations, take your fresh flowers and spices and create a bowl of potpourri instead. Set this in a window so the herbal energies can be carried on gentle winds. In this form, the blend for empathy might be especially nice in a home where tensions are building. Just substitute dried lemon peel for the juice.

Personal Care Products
"Reason clears and plants the wilderness of the imagination to harvest the wheat of art."
— **Austin O'Malley**

The pages of history share numerous products for personal care, many of which can be prepared or found in your kitchen. I know that some readers are a little uneasy about using consumable items on their bodies. For some reason this equates to wearing your refrigerator like a piece of clothing. This need not be so, as historically the pantry provided both sustenance and health to families right through the 1920's.

During earlier time, the kitchen and pantry were a medicine chest for most homes, along with the garden. Many housewives made products from culinary or garden herbs, resulting in much less hazard to the earth. We now have the opportunity to reclaim that knowledge to rebuild the Sacred Self, and save some money besides.

Right from the start you will notice that most of these recipes are not really "mystical" in their application, but very practical. I truly believe that rediscovering our Sacredness also encourages a pragmatic attitude. This outlook recognizes that *anything* can potentially become a spiritual act (or product) by changing our demeanor and approach.

Similarly, a realistic belief system recognizes that there is another side to life, a day-to-day structure, that must be maintained alongside the esoteric. This composition includes how we care for ourselves, our homes and our planet. When our sacred nature becomes a catalyst for positive action, spirituality gets blended with necessity for marvelous results.

Below are some recipes to try. As you prepare the item(s), add other techniques (visualization, prayer, invocation) and symbols that you have used successfully earlier in this text. This will give each product more personalized energy.

Improving your own well-being, or that of your family, in a natural, earth-aware manner is very satisfying. These recipes come from a variety of folk remedials that I regard as fairly accurate. Even so, these should not, under any circumstances, take the place of proper medical attention. If difficulties persist, please consult your physician. Common sense does not indicate a lack of faith or talent on your part; it is a birth-right.

Boils: Place a bunch of parsley soaked in lemon juice on the area over night. This should help bring it out completely.

Burns: Yogurt, butter, margarine or a little lard can cool the effect of a common kitchen burn. This is not, however, recommended if severe blistering or an open wound is involved.

Corns: Every night, apply equal portions of vinegar, lemon juice and baking soda until it disappears.

Cough Syrup: Take one cup of warm honey and add

two quarter-inch slices of fresh ginger root, one clove of garlic, one teaspoon each of rosemary and thyme, 1/2 teaspoon orange rind, and 1/2 teaspoon lemon rind. Keep this in an air-tight container. Use a teaspoon full at a time (straining out the herbs). This mixture also works as a wonderful glaze for poultry and/or an addition to herbal teas.

Deodorizer: A perfect deodorizer for your home and yourself consists of equal proportions of cornstarch and baking soda. Sprinkle this mixture everywhere nasty odors hide. This mix also gets stubborn stains or odors off tile and countertops. For better results add a touch of salt for an abrasive, and lemon juice for shine.

Eyes (puffy): Apply warm tea bags or slices of cucumbers directly to the lid and allow to sit for about 20 minutes.

Eye (wash): 1 tsp. fennel, parsley and baking soda steeped in three cups hot water. Strain and use.

Eye (Sties): Apply steamed cabbage leaf, raw potatoes or tea bags over night.

Feet (sore): Try a soak of warm water, fresh mint leaves and 4-5 whole cloves.

Fish Smells: On your hands, a bit of lemon juice or peel added to your wash water will cut the scent and bring a refreshing aroma into the kitchen. Other citrus fruits also work for this application.

Flu Symptoms: Make a tea with two quarts water and 2 teaspoons each, cinnamon, ginger, honey, lemon, orange, parsley and sage. Take in 1/2 cup proportions about every 1-2 hours. If you find the taste is too strong, add more warm water.

Freckles (to rid): Use equal portions of lemon juice, butter milk, egg white and yogurt beaten together into a mask. Apply and let the mixture dry, then rinse your face thoroughly.

Hair (conditioner): Use one or two eggs as you might your regular shampoo. These will help replace protein. This also works for your pets.

Hair (oily): Prepare a rinse with 2 teaspoons baking soda, 1/4 cup vinegar and a capful of lemon juice, mixed with one can of beer.

Hair (dandruff): Cut up 1/2 cup nettle and one cup parsley in a pint of warm water. To this add 1/2 cup lemon juice, and 2 tablespoons each of rosemary and sage. Cook together for about a half hour, over a low flame then strain. Use after shampooing.
Note: if you have a microwave, I recommend warming this rinse up for 30 seconds before applying. Otherwise it is *very* cold.

Headache: Take a kitchen towel and dampen it. Warm this until it starts to steam in either the oven or microwave (make sure the towel doesn't burn). Apply this when the temperature is tolerable to the area between the forehead and mid cheek.

Indigestion: 1 teaspoon each of dill seed, marjoram, parsley, fennel, anise seed and mint made into a tea with 5 cups boiling water. Strain and use 1/2 cup at a time.

Insect Bites: Place 2 teaspoons full of fresh basil and 2 teaspoons of fresh parsley in 2 cups water. Bring to a low rolling boil. Remove from the heat and strain. Apply the solution directly to the bite to relieve itching and swelling. If irritation continues, soak a clean cloth with the mixture and let it sit on the inflicted area.

Mouthwash: Place one teaspoon each of mint, sage, rosemary, cinnamon and allspice in 3 cups of hot water. Let steep for 30 minutes, then strain and use as desired. Alternatively, chew on a fresh sprig of mint, sage, rosemary or slice of ginger root for similar effect.

Skin (moisturizer): Honey or yogurt applied like a mask. Touches of olive, sesame, almond, peanut or saffron oil applied to the dry skin will also help.

Skin (cleanser): Honey again, only this time add oatmeal! Alternatively, use oatmeal with lemon or orange juice and a little water.

Skin (complexion): Warm one cup of parsley in one cup of water. To this add 1 tablespoon thyme, 1 tablespoon onion juice and 1/4 cup cider vinegar. Be sure to test this on a small area of your skin to make sure it does not irritate. Use as a rinse on oily areas. A gentler solution is made by mixing finely ground corn meal with mashed cooked carrots, juice of one cucumber and a capful each lemon and orange juice. Apply this as a mask for about 30-45 minutes, then rinse thoroughly.

Skin (to tighten & refresh): To two cups hot water add 1 teaspoon each, fennel, mint, rosemary and thyme. Steep for 30 minutes and strain. Rinse your face with this twice a week.

Skin (itching): An oatmeal pack (simply cook a little oatmeal and apply it warm to the area) or bath. Another choice is mixing 1 cup buttermilk with 1/2 cup cider vinegar, 1 teaspoon salt, the juice from one green tomato and a grated raw potato. Apply as a poultice.

Sleep: Make a tea from one teaspoon each of peppermint, honey, rosemary, sage and anise seed in two cups of hot water. Alternatively, hot cocoa or warm milk usually helps.

Swelling: Apply a cloth soaked in 1 cup hot apple cider that has been mixed with 2 teaspoons of sage. Leave on the area for 2 hours.

Toothache: Mix together one drop each of clove oil and vanilla extract. This is a little more palatable than the clove oil straight and children balk less at your use of it.

Personal Diary — April 1987

"Today I became my own situational joke. Here I was, trying to make soap for the first time only to discover myself in the kitchen working over a large iron pot making something that bubbles! My god, shades of William Shakespeare! Despite the humor of the situation, or perhaps because of it, I really found I enjoyed the activity. Much to my surprise, making soap is really fun, especially when I can weave in a spell, stir in a blessed herb, and let it age beneath a full moon to bring out internal radiance with every wash."

Notes

1. The gold coloration in Catholic vestments signifies the priest's position as a representative of the "sun" which also symbolizes God in all his glory.

2. A basic definition of an item or individual's vibration is that of a basic matrix. This matrix defines color, texture, and personality, and gives the item or person a unique feeling and designation that sets it apart.

3. For those who can't readily afford diamonds, Herkimer is an alternative that has all the radiance and appearance of diamonds, but a much more reasonable cost.

4. One lovely bit of folklore tells us that Amber was originally formed from the tears of a setting sun.

5. Animals mark their territory by scenting things. In pets this is easily viewed in cats who rub the sides of their face on people or chairs. In the wild, this is done by spraying trees or rocks with musky scents unique to the animal.

Six:
Friendship, Romance & Love

"Bells of the past whose long forgotten music
fills the wide expanse,
tinging the sober twilight of the present
with the color of romance."
— Francis B. Harte

"She was a little thing called romance"
— James M. Barrie

People endure all manner of indignity to make themselves attractive, to find and secure love, or just to feel more confident about themselves and their relationships. Some of humanities oldest stories center around the brave mortal who must face terrors and tests to win the hand of one desired. With children listening to these kinds of fables down through history, is it any wonder that we allow plastic surgeons to cut our bodies just to be more physically appealing? Is it any wonder that we tolerate chemicals, smells and awkward appearances for hair permanents? Think about it!

Consider fashion trends as a case-in-point. In most cases vogue, not common sense, prevailed. For example, the boned bodices of the Middle Ages quite literally suffocated some women to death. In feudal Japan, the binding of feet was sometimes crippling.

On a less dramatic level, there were the Victorian petty coats and white gloves required by propriety even in a dusty

Mid-Western town. These are not garments of sensibility considering the circumstances. Nonetheless, some of the greatest minds in history have succumb to the fashion bug without even being aware of it! Oh, certainly, there were always a few rebels in any crowd, but they were the minority — a quiet voice for personal expression and coherence in a very rowdy throng.

Humans, are social animals who long to be desired. We have a need to be part of a "pack." This longing manifests itself in many ways, including compliance to externals like fashion. It also exhibits itself in dating, marriage customs and the amazing variety of love magic attempted throughout history.

Since this chapter discusses some of the lengths to which people have gone to ensnare romance (including magical), a word of caution is necessary. I do not condemn love magic as long as it is guided by non-manipulative, positive motivations. Unfortunately, many older love spells and charms were designed without regard for free will or the consequences of hastily contrived power.

The sorrowful tale of Tristan and Isolt is one remarkable archetype to this lesson with tragic results[1]. Here, classical writers remind us powerfully of the frailty of human emotions, and the consequences of toying with same. Love can not be forced or orchestrated if it is to have lasting meaning. Please bear this in mind while you read, or when you attempt any metaphysical workings aimed toward relationships.

Loneliness

I believe loneliness is one of the most common problems plaguing individuals. How many times have you heard someone say "I thought I was the only one who felt that way...", or "I didn't known there were other people like me..." Such phrases, common among our youth, are a strong indication that something is desperately wrong with the way we create and maintain interpersonal relationships and the lines of communication.

At least part of this difficulty developed because of the mobile nature of our society. Miles separate families and friends, making it easier to become lazy. We forget to call or write, and eventually the close rapport fades to a memory. All close relationships need consistent tending for health and longevity.

Another problem is over population. It is easy for people to feel lost in the crowd, like a very small water droplet in a very big sea. We don't want to be overcome by these waves, or washed away with a societal tide. That is why a sense of sacredness is more important today than it ever was before; it sustains firm roots for the foundation of self.

A third, and very common difficulty, are the idealistic expectations of what friendship and love really mean. Anyone can get trapped by the "happily ever after" myth. Here we anticipate that roses and violins accompany each moment of time with another person. Over the long-haul, this expectation is not reasonable.

Love and passion can not last when they rage out of control, nor should our hearts wear blinders to faults that eventually *will* become an issue. A sense of sacredness bridges the gaps between what we hope for, the realities of our situation, and compromise. Love has very discerning ears, observant eyes, helpful hands and a forgiving nature. To integrate this depth of emotion, first you need to define exactly what love means to you.

Personal Diary — August 1994
  "When I listen to my son say I love you, it is different from the words of adults. There are no expectations in his words, no hidden motivations, only a fullness of feeling that we loose somewhere along the way. Our depth of love as adults has been tarnished by years of broken promises, and hundreds of layers of bandages. No wonder we so often feel empty even when we are not alone — we have lost the simplicity of child-like love that trusts completely, believes the best, and is always willing to forgive."

What is Love? (Exercise 1)

For this activity you need either a typewriter, word processor, or lots of writing paper and a pen. When you have a quiet moment, ask yourself the definition of love. What is it that compels you to love another person, or yourself for that matter? What is the difference between the love of a friend and a mate? What makes an individual deserving of your love? How do you describe this baffling human emotion in your own words? Write the answers to these questions out in as much detail as you can.

Review the resulting notes, and consider if your expectations of love are reasonable, or if they are somewhat clouded by overt romanticism, idealistic tendencies, or cynicism. There is nothing wrong with whimsy or caution. The real problems come to bear when we expect to find Mr. or Ms. "perfect."

Except in very rare situations, people regularly discover their mates have human failings that don't fit an ideal.

Prospective life partners and friends are not idle lumps of clay from which to carve out our images of perfection, nor are they handy tools through which to work out our hang ups. Rejecting anyone because of preconceived notions is inherently wrong and unjust. It is similarly unjust to try and recreate others in our own image (even as we've tried to do with God).

Worse yet is when someone is so afraid of closeness that they actually try and find faults that may or may not exist. Generally a relationship experiencing this problem is a pitiful, flurrysome affair that leaves both people wanting. By their paranoid actions, Mr. or Ms. "fear of commitment" neatly cheats themselves and another person of a positive growing experience.

When you reach out to the universe looking for companionship, realize that the answer that you get will not always come in the wrappings expected. "Mr. or Ms. Right" only exist in that stunning form in your dreams. In reality, they are just every-day people, with real limitations, needs and desires of their own.

The Call for Companionship
"And in your eyes, I read companionship."

— Lilla Perry

What is the best way to find long term companionship? Ah, and age-old question to which one of the best answers is to stop trying. Center your attention on your life as it presently exists. Find happiness and fulfillment in yourself, your job, your personal space, your goals and your companions. Around the same time you manage this feat, love follows.

Perhaps this is the Universe's way of exhibiting humor. The minute you think you want nothing to do with another intimate relationship, nine out of ten times someone will appear. This person may be a mysterious stranger, or possibly a long time friend who suddenly seems different to you. Either way, they just materialize like the proverbial rabbit from a hat!

This happened to me personally, and at least a handful of close friends. Nonetheless, there may be moments when loneliness is overwhelming. In these moments, *doing* something positive metaphysically returns the reigns of your fate back into the best possible hands: your own. One possible approach is a non-manipulative "call for companionship."₂ This call can be directed toward friendship or more intimate relationships.

Gather a handful of fresh rose petals on a night when the moon is full, and when a warm southerly₃ wind blows freely. Stand outside in a quiet place and tell the Divine your deepest desires. Describe your vision of a mate in detail, keeping that image strongly in your mind. When you are done, add a phrase like "for the greatest good" so that your prayers do not interfere with another's free will. Then release the flower petals to the winds of change, carrying your energy where it will be received most positively.

Personal Diary — May 1984

"I have met someone new and find he leaves me totally off balance. At a time in my life when I would be content to simply work and enjoy my little apartment alone, he moves in on my reality like a bull in a china shop. There is a boyish

charm that attracts and infuriates me at the same time. I could learn to be more of a kid myself, but I live in an adult world... maybe I'm jealous of his freedom. Maybe I feel more than I'm willing to admit.

If I had ever tried to describe my Mr right, it would have been a nice white-collar guy... steady, dependable... ah, who am I kidding... that would be BORING. Yet I can not help but wonder why him, and why now."

Love Potion #9
"Canst thou not wait for love one flying hour? O heart of little faith."
— **Edmund Gosse**

For another approach to finding and protecting love, we can look to our ancestors for ideas. When perfumes and clothing, gentle words and romantic glances did not ignite or rekindle a heart, people regularly resorted to love potions, spells or other old wives tales. Many medieval Monarchs kept a court magician handy for just such necessities. Commoners probably sought out a village wise person or monk for similar advise. The resulting charms and concoctions must have realized some level of success, or many more people would have lost their heads due to ineffectiveness.

During the reign of Louis XVI of France, Catherine LaVoisin a court Sorceress, was well known for her adept abilities with herbs. Her greatest area of expertise was that of poison and love potions. Sadly, in some cases, both were used on the same individual at different times!

The King's mistresses utilized LaVoisin's talents regularly. Recipes pieced together from this era show that her love elixirs consist of many common spices or plants to the contemporary kitchen. Included in this list are dill, cinnamon, caraway, coriander, nutmeg, rose petals, fennel and celery.

Other customary components for period love potions, but ones that come from different magical chefs, are wine, moonwort, daffodils, ginseng, myrrh, parsley, myrtle, leek or jasmine. In each instance, preparers considered the mixtures alchemical₄ balancing them carefully, thus insuring the most positive and potent results.

To truly appreciate the effort behind these mixtures, one must realize that for the medieval home, many spices and herbs were costly. The smart and profitable merchant would certainly raise his prices for a Lord or King. Yet, no expense was spared if it meant securing affection or an heir.

Today, I generally suggest the use of love potions in three different scenarios. First, create and quaff a specially prepared beverage to improve self-love. Second, when marriage or a long-term commitment are made, share a carefully chosen drink to symbolically strengthen that bond. Third, add these potions to special rituals when pledges to the gods, oneself or others are being renewed. In all instances, people should be aware of what they're drinking. For couples, drinking potions for love or dedication from one cup additionally links their destiny, and shows unity and devotion₅.

To make your own love elixir, try a base of passion fruit juice with a dash of nutmeg and cinnamon. Pour this in a tall glass with two straws, a couple of rose petals for garnish and some whole strawberries, then share it with your companion. Finally, spend some time alone together, reminding yourself of all the reasons you fell in love.

Expressing Emotions

Once you have a stronger understanding about what love should (or should not) be, this discernment also helps define your friendships. People frequently have high aspirations for their close friends because of the deep level of trust exchanged in those relationships. This can kill friendships when expectations prove to be just too much.

As we release our partners and ourselves from oppressive concepts, we need to release our friends too. Part of friendship means loving people with all their faults and weaknesses. From this position of mutual respect, insight and support can fill any gaps.

Once this change in your perceptions begins, you will also notice your ways of communicating change accordingly. Now instead of reproach for perceived failures, you reach out to be understanding. This is the ultimate in positive reinforcement, giving friends and loved ones hopeful energy with which to try again.

Additionally, the way you express emotions will also likely transform. Feelings are very potent, transcending words. For those who have experienced blockage, true love is like an icepick that begins to make cracks in your auric walls. Once a flow is opened, love pours out to totally rejuvenate your relationships.

How do I Express Love (Exercise 2)

Be it friend, family or loved one, expressing our emotions is very important to maintaining intimacy. Having a keen understanding how you represent your feelings, and why you express them in certain way, is critical to any changes you hope to make. After all, a problem is hard to fix if you can't find the source.

For this activity, have a healthy amount of paper handy for free-flow writing. Think about your close interpersonal relationships including one or two friendships, a serious relationship, and those between you and your family. Make notes on the ways you have shown your love to them over the years. Are you a hugger? Do you talk about your feelings? Do you give gifts as a means of communication?

Next consider how your parents expressed their love to you. Do you find any of these traits in yourself? If so, are they characteristics that you like, or do you want to change them to become more suitable to sacred beauty? All of us, in some form or another, repeat the communication patterns we learned as children. Not all of those standards were good ones.

In some instances, we simply accepted that the world we experienced as youth is a verity; simply the "way" things are done. Child abuse is one lamentable example of this, with battered children growing up and becoming violent with their own children. Sacred self-discovery offers us a chance to break those types of negative patterns. Here, we choose what to integrate or segregate from that learning experience.

Self-love, and the love of others frees us to find our own Path and define our own truths. Old behaviors get cast off for something more positive and life affirming. For achieving the Sacred Self, shedding the old skin is nothing less than vital.

Altering Behavior Patterns
"The enchanting miracles of change"
— Michael Field

Are you unhappy with the way you think about, or

express, your emotions? Are their portions of your personality that hold you back? Nearly everyone I know answers yes to one, or both, of these questions. The most difficult aspect of Sacred Beauty's quest is discovering the common denominators to resolve these quandaries.

Life long habits will not change over night. Once you're aware of them, however, it's easier to make purposeful efforts toward changing that cycle. If, for example, you put yourself down, stop and think before speaking. Try to find positive ways of expressing self-awareness. Say you've just finished a huge meal that you slaved over. Instead of asking sheepishly if dinner was ok, pat yourself on the back and proclaim the meal a success.

This may seem a little arrogant, but loved ones grow rapidly tired of someone who constantly demeans themselves. It's like saying that their love was ill-chosen, that they should be with someone more "worthwhile." So, unwittingly, you insult not only yourself, but them as well.

In sharing our life with others, it is best to begin by being content with ourselves. Acknowledge your faults, but still believe in your worthiness. By so doing, accepting other's faults becomes much easier. From this substructure, relationships can blossom in honesty and security, blossoming direct from the heart.

The Declaration (Exercise 3)

Each day for one year, look at yourself in a mirror and repeat the following phrases with conviction.

"I am."

"I am worthy"

"I am worthy to give."

"I am worthy to give and to receive."
"I am worthy to give and to receive love."

This activity is very similar to the self affirmations in Chapter 3. The difference here is the building process. Believe in the words and believe in yourself. Allow each phrase to bring renewed confidence and conviction.

Alternatively, you can use this activity to support friends or family members by changing the "I am" to "You are," and speaking the phrases to each other. In this instance, eye contact is exceedingly important. By keeping that contact, your partner will sense the true emotions beneath your words. You may also change the expressions for more personalized goals. Here are two examples:

To Another Person
"You are."
"You are beautiful."
"You are beautiful and Sacred."
"You are beautiful, Sacred and loved."
"You are beautiful, Sacred, and I love you."

Spoken Together
"We are"
"We are united"
"We are united and strong"
"We are united, strong and blessed"
"We are united and blessed in each others arms".

This exercise may also prove helpful for people who are uncomfortable with expressing their emotions. First, they learn to communicate important feelings with themselves, then slowly move toward sharing feelings more freely with others.

Changing Techniques (Exercise 4)

I am someone who shows her emotions through what I do, not what I say. My partner is just the opposite, causing no end of miscommunication between us. When you discover yourself in a similar situation, one of the best solutions is finding a mutually agreeable middle ground from which to build.

For instance, if you have a friend or companion who needs physical contact for assurance, make an effort to hug them daily. If they are a life partner, give them a morning kiss. Statistics show that individuals who are kissed before work actually have longer life spans. Continue reinforcing your feelings until the gesture becomes natural. Both people will benefit from the process.

Also observe how often you actually say the words "I love you." Ponder how long it has been since you surprised a friend with flowers, a good book or a gourmet meal. All of these things, no matter how small, can really make a quality difference in rapport. The attempts will be even more meaningful if it is something you aren't apt to do normally. Extending extra efforts out of consideration rarely goes unnoticed.

For "acquaintances" a slightly different technique must be considered. One of the greatest courtesies you can extend to others is thoughtfulness regarding personal space. Another is being mindful of any physical needs that person may have. Finally, there is marvelous warmth and simplicity in a "hello" smile.

With so many people living in urban environments, the need for personal space has increased geometrically. Have you ever noticed how little eye contact is made in tight elevators or subways, or how people try to etch out a niche for themselves in these places? That is an outward expression of discomfort with close proximity to other peoples auras!₆

As we become more aware of this, we can quite naturally make a little more room for those folk who are a little claustrophobic. For that matter, we can offer our seat on the bus to the woman with a young baby, a man bearing a cane, or someone who looks overtly weary. Perception, when followed by considerate actions, is a free gift. Pass it on! Make someone's day a little better by expressing Sacred Beauty in your own way.

Personal Diary — July 1994

"Kaz brought over his new fiancé today, Melanie. What a lovely girl — full of joy, intelligence and she even puts up with his youthful zeal! That alone should make her a saint. Mel mentioned to me that she needed a costume for an SCA₇ event in a few weeks. I remembered having a dress in storage for the last few years that would look absolutely stunning on her. Sure enough, it fit just right, and flowed all around her like a cloud.

When I told her to keep it, you would have thought I'd given her a bar of gold. She felt awkward and overjoyed all at the same time. Then I explained to her that 13 years ago someone had given me my first medieval dress and I never forgot that kindness. Now her job, and her thanks to me, was to carry on the tradition!"

Within The Heart
"Heaven comes down to touch us when we find ourselves safe in another's heart."

— A. Whitman

Once we have build a relationship, the next part seems almost as difficult as was finding love, that of maintenance. Relationships do not just naturally go smoothly. Humans are too unique, too persnickety and too territorial not to get our knickers in a twist occasionally. When this occurs, it no longer matters how much we love each other, or how long that relationship has survived; all that matters is who's right or wrong. Unfortunately, that could be both individuals or neither!

No one ever said that being a spiritually aware person would make relationships effortless. A balanced awareness and a stronger tolerance for other people's individuality helps, but it doesn't solve everything. The garden of love has to be tended persistently to keep out the weeds of jealousy, wrath, resentment, bitterness and selfishness.

Maintaining Love (Exercise 5)

What do you consider essential for maintaining the quality of love? Consider tackling this question with your life mate or a close friend who will be really honest. Your responses may immediately reveal certain repetitive problems in that relationship.

Say, for example, you feel your partner should help with daily chores to show his or her understanding of your needs. If you never directly expressed that desire to your partner, they may be surprised by this information. Perhaps they think you enjoy those errands, or are very picky about the way they get completed. Consequently, they stay out of your way. By sharing your disappointment in the lack of domestic partnership, you may very quickly clear up one disparagement.

Other good questions to answer during this activity include:

* *How much private time does a couple need to spend together daily (or weekly) to maintain the quality of their communications?*

* *Does a couple need to have common friends or is it ok to have separate groups with whom you each go out? If so, how often is it appropriate to "party" without your mate?*

* *How do children change the relationship equation? How can you find ways (if considering a child) to maintain tenderness once a baby arrives? If you already have children, how can you rediscover any lost intimacy?*

* *Does a couple need to have common hobbies? If so, how much of their private time should those hobbies encompass?*

* *Are sit-down, family dinners important to maintaining family ties? What about TV — do you feel the amount of viewing time helps or hurts your intimacy? The computer? Video games?*

* *If there was one activity you could get your partner to share with you, what would it be and why? Have you told them that you want them to be part of this special endeavor?*

Likewise if there was one activity you could get your partner to give up, what would it be and why?

* *If you could choose one household chore for your partner every week, which one would it be? Have you asked if they would share this duty?*

* *How does your job or that of your mates/friends effect your relationship? How much time do you spend talking about work at home?*

* *How many "problems" in your relationship are actually difficulties between the two of you and how many are external pressures over which you have no control? Should the latter be allowed to disrupt household harmony?*

These are only a few thoughtful questions that have come up in my own relationships. To these, I'm certain you can add several more that pertain more directly to your circumstances. Throughout this activity it is essential that you are totally honest, caring and constructive with your answers. You are building or rebuilding certain foundations in your relationship. Affirmation and cooperation are the two key elements for success.

Coping with Jealousy

Jealousy is a terribly self-serving emotion. It silently tells your partner that they are not worthy of your trust. It doesn't matter if you're jealous of a job, their success, or a partner's close friends. When this feeling gets out of control, it can spark an angry fire that destroys relationships.

If you are a jealous person, begin by understanding this emotion for what it is. The desire for assured love has turned into fear of being alone. This causes "clutching," like a child who tries to take back a toy from a playmate.

People are not toys or possessions. When individuals choose to share their lives, they come with their own circle of friends and activities that don't always mesh perfectly together. Neither should have to give up their hobbies just to prove devotion to another person. In fact, when you release your companion to do what they enjoy, they will love you even more.

The same holds true for old friends. These people are NOT competition for your mate's affection. They are just people who love that individual as you do. I remember my best friend crying on my sisters' shoulder when I got married, sensing a kind of loss that wasn't easily expressed. I felt it too, but our friendship still endures with some minor variations appropriate to new situations. In fact our husbands have become good friends as well. This would not have happened if jealousy had gotten in the way.

It seems Jonathan Livingston Seagull had some valuable advise when he said "if you love something let it go." This builds trust — a sense that you understand your partners pleasure in their pastimes and friends. It also makes the bond of love one which is comfortable instead of constraining.

The only time a question of "freedom" should arise is when you feel, somehow, you are being neglected or side-stepped. Frequently a short, honest discussion will clear up a lot of misgivings in this case. You can't expect people to correct a problem if they don't know one exists in your eyes.

You likewise can't always expect that your partner will

understand it to be a problem, even when you explain it to them. This is part of the human equation that takes time, effort, sagacity and patience to work out. In those moments, let your Sacred Self shine brightly from within to fill your words with compassion and constructive options. Then listen to the response with ears of discernment.

Personal Diary — January 1993
"This should be the happiest time of my life. My first book just hit the bookshelves. Yet instead of joy I find some concern. A close friend and my husband both have expressed some jealousy over my achievement instead of sharing my jubilation. Somehow they feel they have to compete, or share their lives with that book, its readers and me.

In some ways, I know they are right. My life is about to change in ways I can't even begin to envision. Similarly, there were a lot of sacrifices made by everyone close to me to get this thing to press. I have spent more hours at the library and in front of the computer than at home over the last year! Yet, I am immensely grateful for their help and support, and hope they grow to see that thankfulness."

The Green-Eyed Monster (Exercise 6)
One way to release jealousy is with your companions' help. For this activity you need a length of good string (about 5 yards) and a pair of scissors. Wrap one half of the string around your waist, and the other half around your partners waist. Leave slack in between so you can stand facing each other.

Take turns cutting a piece of the string away, likewise cutting away any unhealthy feelings or ties between you.

Name each one of these strings out loud as you cut. For example:

"I release my jealousy towards your job, knowing you work to help ease the financial burdens of our lives."

"I release my expectations of you which are too demanding of your personal time, especially when you need rest."

"I release my anger that was aimed towards you when you wanted to visit your friends. I was being selfish"

This can be a tremendously liberating experience that will probably bring many tears along the way. Let them flow. Crying has a healing effect on the body and spirit, and also releases pent up tensions.

Consider your words carefully before this mini-ritual, knowing they will deeply impact your partner and that relationship that day forward. Do not release anything with word that you aren't willing to follow by deed. Take things one step at a time, growing together, freeing each other, then finally flying side by side.

The Fury Within (Exercise 7)

Whoever said 'love means never having to say you're sorry' was full of unmitigated crap. No matter how good a relationship is, there are bound to be disagreements and even down-n-out temper tantrums. Afterwards, when the dust clears along with heads, you can re-approach the whole matter and hopefully iron things out. Even so, there are emotional scars to consider.

Arguments leave us feeling guilty for allowing fury to

rage out of control, or for making unnecessarily hurtful statements. Yet there is also assuagement, knowing the majority of the problem is out in the open; knowing at last you have spoken your mind. Somewhere between the pain and relief, balm must be applied to heal both people, and to the relationship itself.

The moment of forgiveness is a point of restoration, not a moment to quibble over who won. Leave the idea of winners and losers out of your relationships. Intimacy is not a place for competition or rivalry. When arguments erupt and feelings are injured, both people loose something, no matter whose opinion was functionally correct.

To help the healing process along, everyone involved should begin by apologizing. Not because anyone was necessarily "wrong," but because that relationship suffered. Similarly, if there were other people around who got caught in the cross-fire, apologize to them too. There is nothing more uncomfortable than silently watching friends quarrel.

Next, take a deep breath, shake hands or hug, then sit down like rational adults and really talk. Discuss the pressures and tensions that lead to the argument. Talk about the hard day at work, lack of sleep or disagreeable sales clerk who ticked you off earlier. Communicate about the "whys" of being upset, not just the central issue. Then find a compromise.

Finally, find a disposable object to symbolize your combined anger and resentment. Together, break that item and bury it$_8$, figuratively signaling the death to that whole subject. This burial is an unspoken promise by all parties to leave that issue in the past. Consider planting a bush, flower or tree over that spot, so beauty may grow where only anger had been sown before.

From this moment forward, allow a new day to begin where the past no longer shadows your love. Repeat this exercise any time such difficulties arise. Make the process of maintaining your love a mutual affair.

The Sacred "We"

"There were three, you and I, and we. Without you there would be less than one."
— **Leonard Nimoy, "You and I"**

It takes most couples years to achieve that elusive balance that makes for predominantly happy interactions. Marriage, commitment, or living together is not, in itself, the whole answer to creating a unified whole from two separate individuals. That is only a first step in a long journey — a journey that continues every day you spend together.

As each individual grows and changes, their relationships also change. Because of this, it is important to periodically pause and consider this growth and what it means. Take time to assimilate transformation and its effects, especially on intimate levels.

Sometimes these reevaluations are difficult. When people grow apart, it is not always easy to accept. Sacred beauty uses understanding and compassion as a guide, so this situation does not become a tragedy. Instead, recognize the benefits of that relationship up to this juncture, even If it can't be the same in the future.

On a happier note, some couples discover that they are far better together after some years. The maturity of knowledge, wisdom and shared experience allowed the trees of their lives to intertwine and flower. Yes, problems still exist within and without. I'd be lying if I said there weren't. The external ones are circumstantial and will fade only to be replaced by other sociological pressures and day-to-day happenstance. The internal ones will be brought to bear, worked out, then be likewise replaced. Nonetheless, two Sacred Beings do not focus all their time and attention on the negatives. Be it friends or life partners, they carefully balance these with the joy, productivity and pleasure in each other's company.

While this story book doesn't always end "happily ever after," it is mostly content. Within a relationship where two souls dwell in harmony, something powerful is created. They give birth to the Sacred We. It is from this empowered seed that truly incredible expressions of adoration, passion and devotion blossom to sustain love until death takes us, or the world ends[9].

Notes

1. Isolt of the White Hand was a beautiful maiden promised to a foreign King to insure peace between two warring nations. Isolt was given a special potion that, when consumed, would allow her to look upon this king and love him completely. Unfortunately, during the journey it was accidentally quaffed. Tristian and Isolt gazed at each other and fell in love. Both people being aware of what happened, and wishing to remain true to King and country, gave up their happiness for the better good. Isolt still married the foreign king, but their love never faded.

2. Manipulation of free will in the esoteric realms is considered completely improper. Those who try to tamper with other peoples feelings have little regard for the sanctity of life.

3. I have chosen the southern winds for this bit of folk magic because of their warm nature. Southern winds bring a change in weather or, in this case, our attitudes.

4. Alchemy was the forerunner to modern chemistry, being dedicated to finding a formula for making gold, and to find the elixir of eternal youth. The story of Ponce De Leon probably had some foundation in Medieval Alchemical principals.

5. In Celtic regions, it was common to see groups of people eating and drinking in a circle with the leader of the group and his guests at the center. These communal feasts often featured one cup, passed sunwise in the direction of their rituals, as a public show of their unity. Gypsies also often used one cup in marriage rites, as does Judaism.

6. The aura is basically your own physical energy, most commonly experienced in body temperature. Some mystics can actually see auras as a patterned sphere of colored light around individuals. This pattern takes on unique texture, taste and even sound that either mingles or clashes with other energy fields nearby.

7. The SCA (Society for Creative Anachronism) is a 25 year old, worldwide organization dedicated to the study and reenactment of medieval arts and sciences. They hold events on a year round basis, do educational demonstrations for schools, and hold lectures and workshops to try and reclaim the "lost" talents of this era. To get more information, write: SCA, Box 360789, Milpitas CA 95036-0789.

8. If you don't have a yard, a small indoor plant pot will do. Alternatively, if the item is biodegradable and in small enough pieces, you can flush it down the toilet.

9. This last sentence is part of many contemporary wedding vows.

Seven:
Beauty, Sexuality And New-Age Ideals

"Ideals are like stars; you will not succeed in touching them with your hands. But like the seafaring man on the desert of waters, you choose them as your guides, and following them you will reach your destiny."

— Carl Schurz

"Behold the bright countenance of truth in the quiet and still air of delightful studies."

— John Milton

We do not live on islands, neatly secluded away from the persuasions of our communities. To say that we are not biased at least somewhat by this community would be naive. One only need examine the level of trust exhibited in a city versus a rural setting to discover environmentally generated concepts at work.

Our world is in a constant state of metamorphosis on every level; it is inescapable. Technology and social ideals change far more quickly than most people adapt to them. This leaves many of us, even those with years of spiritual insight, somewhat confused as to what role the Sacred Self plays in this transforming drama called life.

Among the modifications of great concern are sexuality and sensuality. There exists increasing peer pressure on our youths for outward expressions of maturity (for which they may or may not be prepared). Among adults and teenagers alike, varying gender-specific roles creates confusion and uncertainty. Add to this an era where diseases like Aids wreak havoc on bodies, and the sum of the equation is emotional chaos wherein the Sacred Self yearns for expression.

Obviously, with sexually transmitted disease causing deaths every day, a sense of prudence is increasingly necessary. Yet, at what cost? Do we forego physical expression, except when accompanied by a doctors note, altogether? To my mind, the entire question is like a teeter-totter with abstinence on one side, intimacy on the other and notions of attractiveness, and the need to be desired, balanced aimlessly in between.

Thus, reclaiming the sanctity of the body is one essential building block for the Sacred Self. We then hold this particular brick in place with the mortar of understanding — realizing what beauty truly represents in metaphysical terms. If all we know of loveliness is what the media presents to us, then it is high time we look elsewhere for a healthy, balanced vision. As cliche as it may sound, beauty really does come from within. I know some physically stunning people who, on a one-to-one level, are completely unattractive. Like a fancy Barbie and Ken doll, the plastic facade only holds up from a distance.

By comparison, the Sacred Self is not artificial. It is born from a deep awareness of the soul's uniqueness and importance as co-creator with the Divine. This energy, once accepted and integrated, can literally alter external images because you carry yourself differently. Confidence, centering, and Ky_1 (as the Orientals call it) become honed and ready to meet the world. Those around you can not help but notice this change.

Instead of grasping at relationships like the life line of a boat, you rest calmly at the shore and allow love to find you. Instead of offering your body in hopes of securing romance, you choose to wait and express that depth of emotion to someone really special. This is not puritanical, but an external expression of knowing your own resplendence and worthiness. No matter what modern morality claims is fashionable, your body is sacred, your emotional well being is sacred and YOU ALONE should be the person deciding when and how to express intimacy.

Unfortunately no guru or textbook can give you a perfect guideline on knowing the "right time." So, the Sacred Self must learn again to believe the voice of conscious. The more we heed that internal wisdom, the more it proves itself right. Start trusting yourself again today.

The Beauty Within me (Exercise 1)

It is a rare person who can look themselves straight in the eyes and say without hesitation, "I am beautiful." Partially, we feel this statement to be boastful or egotistical, but when voiced with the right attitude, it is neither. If you haven't begun already, now is the time to think in terms of beauty as an ideal, not a commodity. Focus your time and energies on the brightness of spirit; that quality of being, purely motivated actions, lovingly contrived reactions . . . the Divine you.

For this activity you will need to find one object or picture that, to you, best represents the ideal of beauty. The simpler the image, the deeper emotional response to that likeness, the better this exercise will work.

A week before actually performing the following

visualization, leave the object or picture in a predominant place. If possible, take it with you like a portable nick-knack so that a vivid, three dimensional portrait of it appears in your mind even when your eyes are closed. Each time you see that object, consider the meaning of ideal beauty, and what it represents to you on the deepest levels of your awareness.

Then, before starting the visualization, insure yourself of some quiet, uninterrupted time. Put on soft, centering₂ music that reminds you of a safe, warm haven. Have a full length mirror nearby, get completely undressed and find a very comfortable position for yourself, be it sitting, lying down, or whatever.

Next, consciously slow your breathing a little. Take a few deep, cleansing breaths that help you relax. Allow your tensions to flow away with each exhale, then draw in vibrant energy when you inhale. Some people find it effective to see this in their minds' eye like white light pouring into them, and dark muddy ooze moving away.

Now, bring a vision of your chosen object or picture clearly into your mind. Allow all the phrases and feelings associated with that object, and specifically Sacred Beauty, to fill every cell of your being as you actively imagine it. As your emotions swell, allow the vision to likewise grow larger until it expands to the point where your entire body, including the aura, is encompassed by loveliness.

In your imagination, see how the picture of splendor does not overshadow you, but is translucent so that you and the ideal merge with ease. Reach out your hands and stroke the edges of the image while drawing it toward you. Hold it close like a welcome friend, and absorb all the special attributes associated with the object into your Sacred Self.

Now, open your eyes and look into the mirror. Notice the slight glow of energy that floats all around you. This is the radiance of your soul. Write down your feelings in your diary, especially how your perceptions of self have changed. Repeat any time you feel your sense of Spiritual Beauty waning[3].

Personal Diary — July 1988
"I never completely realized until recently how hung-up I am about my own body. Even during the hottest of summers, I still want a small nighty or bit of sheet to cover myself... yet cover from whom? When I'm dressing, I notice my eyes shy away from the mirror as if not to stare rudely at some unnamed indiscretion. Why? What ever made me feel that the naked body was anything to be ashamed of?

I watch my son, and at this age there are no such preconceptions. Children run happily bare-bottomed at the beach, gleeful for the freedom from diapers and other clothing. They exhibit no shame, no remorse, only gentle acceptance."

Defining Relationships
The world, uncertain, comes and goes. The lover, rooted, stays."
— Ralph Waldo Emerson

In the last chapter we discussed personal relationships in depth. Sometimes it is difficult to define exactly when relationships change from one phase into another. When does an acquaintance become a friend? When should friends become lovers? When do lovers become life mates? There is no clear-cut, coloring book lines to answer these questions in our society, and sometimes not even in our own minds.

The dictionary defines an acquaintance as someone with whom you are familiar, but not closely tied. This might include co-workers, a fellow commuter, and even your bus driver. Friendship is more elusive.

Friends are interpreted as "helpers" who also have mutual affections and respect for you. Within this boundary, the trust friendship inspires makes the possibilities almost boundless. Under the right circumstances the potential for romance or intimacy can dance teasingly on the edge of our awareness.

In other scenarios there is no chance of romantic interludes, uncomplicating friendships tremendously. There is nothing harder than telling a friend (or a lover) that you don't want anything more than kinship. This step can irreparably damage the lines of communication due to awkwardness, pain or embarrassment. If this has happened to you, ask yourself if that friendship is important enough to work past the problems. If you achieve this without too much heart ache, the resulting friendship will be lasting, honest and potent for both people.

Personal Diary — Summer 1987

"There are moments when we see each other, look at each other, and know without a word what's on our minds. There are such strong ties sometimes that it still hurts to see him with his wife, even though I am happily married. I guess it's true that love doesn't die... it simply changes form to be more acceptable to the transformation in human interactions. But then again, if it did fade, that would make love into something as transient and meaningless as a casual hello from a stranger.

I have finally accepted the fact that there will always be a place in my heart for him; not one of lover, teacher or confidant, but simple friendship born from years of understanding, allowing each other to grow, letting go, and coming back ... always knowing if we need each other, that warmth is still there to fill the gaps."

Sometimes friends become lovers out of mutual loneliness, but such interactions have to be kept in perspective. Each person should hold no expectations, and must recognize that an end to the intimacy could come very quickly if one person or the other gets "involved." My only word of caution is that the resulting emotional ties, no matter how liberated we think ourselves, can be hard to break.

Don't risk a good friendship just because you're horny or need to affirm that you're still alive though a physical act. If you can't separate something purely corporeal from your heart, don't enter into this type of physical expressions. Everyone's peace of mind will benefit.

Also, don't feel guilty if decide to say "no" to a friend's request for intimacy. Saying "no," in this case, means saying "yes" to what honors your Sacred Self. You might feel a tinge of regret because of the other persons loneliness, but that is not reason enough to jeopardize the whole friendship. Most times, people who are truly good friends will understand and respect your decision. In the moments when they don't, you must trust yourself enough to know that you have made the best, most honest choice you could.

Sorting it Out (Exercise 2)

Make a list of all the people in your life. Beside each

name give a brief description of how you see that person fitting into your life today, one year from now, five years from now and twenty five years from now. Some of your observations may prove startling.

Some people may show potential, in your mind, for commitments in the future. Others might be envisioned as transient — likely to disappear after only a short amount of interaction. Keep this list for a year, and review it on your birthday. See just how perceptive you were, or how you perhaps misjudged some people. If you like, make another list for next year at this time. The list is a very insightful tool in gauging gut instincts about your social circle.

Long Term Relationships

Last but not least in this jumbled puzzle is the long-term intimate relationship. While it may sound radical, I do not believe humankind was necessarily meant to be monogamous. This particular trait is not common to most animal species, and may very well be something thrust upon us by a Patriarchal, Christian mind-set.

In old Arabic homes, a man would take several wives. In this setting, the women became help-mates to each other, sharing responsibilities for the whole. This afforded them more personal time, gave the man more attention and security, and certainly gave the women strong companions and allies. It also provided assurances of children and heirs. In truth, this was but one of many pre-Christian cultures that thrived using a multi-mated or extended household system.

I know there have been times in my life when I would have reveled in such an atmosphere, needing someone to understand and help without sexual expectations. Actually, I have more than once told my husband that I wanted a wife! Since we do not live in a society that approves of multiple partners, how well this theory would function in practice today can only be conjectured. About the only evidence we have for potential success stories are in communal homes or communities, which often receive negative press and pressure from their neighbors.

Thus, I think that many problems in extended relationships might ease with the understanding that there may be a small part of the human creature which still yearns for the wildness — the freedom and the advantages that more than one mate offers, at least in our fantasies. To illustrate, if one looks approvingly at a person of the opposite sex while with their mates, it is not necessarily an insult. It may not even be an exhibition of desire, but instead a genuine appreciation. Remember, if they stop looking — check their pulse!

Or, if a person is flirtatious with people after many years of marriage, it may be a way of affirming their self-worth through the eyes of someone new. A little verbal banter can be quite flattering and inspiring from the right people. Outside the setting where we spend most of our time, flirting promotes a renewed sense of attractiveness. Then, all that remains is taking that refreshed awareness home.

Similarly, when an affair does happen, no matter how painful it might seem, at least consider the multi-partner theory as part of the explanation. It may not "fix" the other internal problems, but it can calm you enough to positively tackle the situation. In no way does this concept excuse deceit. It simply gives us a tool towards handling a very touchy problem with more insight.

Redefining Terminology

"A single word has sometimes lost or won empires — even less."

— George Payne Rainsford-James

Sex is not simply a casual roll in the hay for most people. While there are some who can seemingly divorce their heart from other passions, humans connect a great deal of meaning to the sexual act itself, let alone all the preludes. So, when one person gives an uncommitted "I desire you, and another person interprets that as "I love you," real predicaments occur.

At least part of this difficulty begins with the way we talk about love, sex, genders, races, bodily parts, etc. Our language is genuinely reflective of common perceptions. It seems very difficult for most people to talk about private parts of the body without using slang or childish terms. This is because we are, for the most part, a rather prudish lot who are not comfortable with the sensuality of others, or even our own body.

Similarly, somewhere along the way the respectful terms of "Ma'am", "Mister", "Sir" and "Mrs" faded into near oblivion. I find myself cringing when local children call me "Trish" instead of "Mrs. Telesco." To me, this represents the prevailing lack of manners and respect for adults among our young adults. While I might sound like Emily Post here, when those terms were in common usage our society was far more polite. Agreed, it was also less liberated, but that doesn't mean that we can't find a way to have freedom and courtesy in the same conversations.

The best way to achieve this is using inclusive, nonoffensive terms. Try and find positive, possibly older phrases, which describe the same things in less diminutive manners. Use the proper terms for physical parts. There is nothing "dirty" about those words. In the process, you will probably find the way you think about others, yourself and matters of intimacy changing to meet your new language skills. I also think the reaction you get from those around you will be very enlightening.

Linguists have documented how words influence and reflect the ideology of both individuals and cultures. Words carry power of which we are often unaware. Indeed, the same words spoken by two different people can have drastically different effects depending on tone, delivery and environment.

So it remains for us to remember to be sensitive with our words, tempering them with forethought. As spiritual people who are actively seeking enlightenment and self actualization, we carry the responsibility for the potency of our discourse squarely on our shoulders. Speak with the same consideration as you wish from others, and you can not help but be successful.

The Sexual/Sexual Sacred Self

"The omnipresent processes of sex, as it is woven into the whole texture of our man's or woman's body, is the pattern of all the process of our life."
— Havelock Ellis

In the beginning, humankind did not perform sex for pleasure. It was an animal instinct fulfilled in animalistic manner. While a certain amount of release and residual enjoyment was found in this activity, it more importantly rendered a function in society; that of insuring the continuance of the race.

Then, as ancient civilizations grew, the individual pursuit of pleasure expanded, including the sensual realms. We are creatures who need touch; whose understanding of the world around them is often based on our immediate reactions to a specific stimulus. If it "felt good," it was repeated. If something hurt, it was avoided. Much like a child learning about fire, humankind now was discovering their limits and boundaries including those of intimacy.

From then until now the exploration continued. With each new era, new ideas, technology and social changes swept away the "old school." It could not, however, sweep away the influence or earlier ideology of the elders of a community. So, a mish-mash of feelings erupted with every wave of civilization about sexuality, sensuality and what they should or should not mean.

Since the Sacred Self is a unique creature, we need to be aware of these strictures, but not necessarily impeded by them. While I am not an advocate of anti-social behavior, some of the exacting conduct expected by factions of our society are not only unrealistic, but sometimes unsafe and harmful in the long-run.

One good example comes from a recent article (August 1993) of the Wall Street Journal where a writer was espousing natural birth control, specifically for strict Catholics. Ok on the surface, right? Ok until you consider over population and starvation. Alright until we learn that this writer's wife could die from another pregnancy. This particular example is not meant to point figures at the Catholic church solely. Instead it is but one illustration of puritanical and/or patriarchal ideals run amok — even in an age of reason!

Sensual Self Discovery (Exercise 4)

The word sensual does not have to be hedonistic. We are all sense-ual beings, interpreting life from our five major faculties; namely sight, taste, hearing, smell and feeling. These senses help us to learn, and allow us to experience life with multidimensional fullness.

So, when the Sacred Self begins to discover a sensual nature, physicality is but one part of a much greater picture. Sensual awareness helps in many facets of life other than sex. For example, learning to be better listeners, be more observant, to smell the change of weather in the air . . . all of these things attune our lives to the natural rhythm of the universe. From here, sensing the cadence of our pleasure is a small step, but one difficult for many.

Before moving into more intimate realms where we will define what is enjoyable for us, start with simpler matters of learning to be more aware. Go outside and listen closely to the sounds you hear and those you don't. Taste the air, smell the dirt and hear concrete beneath your feet. Come to know the world through all your senses.

Watch where the sun rises daily, and feel the incredible comfort in the warm beams greeting you. Make mental note of slight differences in the sky, activity of pets, or even a mysterious scent on the wind. Slowly, over a year's time, your perception grows and matures to where it is natural to extend your senses and recognize the signs they provide.

Once you reach this point, it is easier to direct this same scrutiny toward yourself, and specifically toward intimate moments. There is nothing wrong with discussing the touches, the words, and the techniques that fulfill you physically with your partner. In fact, most people would be relieved to have this kind of openness instead of the awkward, guess-work errors that often occur.

If you are uncertain about exactly what feels good, then experiment! Your body is not a dirty thing, and you are certainly not being self abusive pleasing yourself. Slide your hand across the curve of your skin. Feel the texture of various fabrics to find those that excite a tingle of anticipation. Fantasize a bit.

In some ways, learning to play with your own body again is like being an open minded, adventurous child. For this activity to be really be effective you have to toss aside puritanical strictures for a moment and enjoy the excitement of innovation! Discover for yourself what makes you happy, then share that marvelous treasure with someone who loves you. Both people will benefit.

Personal Diary — undated

"I never had sex until I was 21. Thankfully the first experience was with someone who didn't laugh at me for not knowing even the basics. See, we never spoke openly about such matters in my family until I was too old and too embarrassed to admit that while I knew the biology of sex, I certainly had no idea about the tender details.

This man taught me to explore, to let loose a bit. But when he was gone, something inside of me clammed back up inside that safe, non-physical shell once more. Pleasurable sex from that point on equated to opening myself again, becoming vulnerable, giving something of myself that I wanted to hold back so I wouldn't get hurt."

1996 Afterthought — To this day I still find this partially true. Even with my husband I have not been able to totally relinquish that need for control; the need to keep one small corner of my heart to myself. I don't know if this is "right" or "wrong", but I know he senses the holding back, and wonders if it's his fault. Slowly we are working on this together, but it may be a long road traveled.

Images of Intimacy (Exercise 5)

Along with the confusion that results from misinterpreting sensuality to only meaning something sexual, there is an additional bewilderment about what defines intimacy. Can two people talking be an intimate moment even if they never touch? Can glances be intimate? Hugs?

Intimacy is not interpreted so much by an action as by the feeling behind that action. One person can give a friendly pat on the back and inspire nothing, while another generates whole worlds of feeling from a simple smile. The basic difference lies in that person's intentions and our interpretation of those intentions. The last portion of this equation is where many communication problems begin.

Humans have a tendency to project their own faults or wishes onto those within their daily circle. This causes tremendous moments of awkwardness where people feel misconstrued. So, understanding our feelings about intimacy becomes important to preserving sacredness within ourselves and our relationships.

First and foremost each individual must determine the correct level of intimacy for each situation or person that they encounter. You will behave differently with close friends than you do with lovers, for example. Similarly, one would not

French kiss a cousin, this being a total breach of personal space considering that person's relationship to you.

For this exercise, simply make notes for yourself in your diary of those people with whom you are intimate. Then consider what ways you share that intimacy with them. How is it expressed? Are you totally happy with that expression? Do you feel it is sufficient, obtrusive or lacking? If it is not sufficient, how could you work toward making a positive change without hurting someone's feelings?

To illustrate, if you have a dear old aunt who always hovers, how do you broach that subject? They are trying to express their amity in a personally uncomfortable way. Yet, if you bring it up, how much intimacy will it cost? Will they then feel awkward whenever around you, wondering if they're "too close?"

These are not easy questions or subjects to introduce, but they are necessary. If handled with discretion, adjustments can be made by both people that honor the Sacred Self. Better yet, such discourse can revolutionize your interactions, and sometimes even resurrect a relationship you thought hopeless.

Defining Sexual Strictures (Exercise 6)

With intimacy and sensuality out of the way, the next step is determining sexual boundaries. The world sometimes portrays different sexual standards than those we find comfortable. This depiction places pressure on people, especially teenagers, to identify themselves with a group, an ideal, and sexual activity for which they may or may not be ready.

Sex is not "cool" or "mature" or something that makes you any more attractive. It is an expression of emotion, a sharing of body and spirit, between two people. Even between two consenting adults there are limits. When the voice within says "no," listen! Ignoring intuitive guides usually leads to nothing but guilt, confusion and other related troubles.

Take the time to decide what is best for you and your body, and stick to that guideline in all your relationships without fail. If it helps, make notes about these rules in your diary. When someone does not respect these guidelines, they also do not recognize the Sacredness of your soul. At this juncture it is perfectly acceptable to stalwartly declare your personal intimacy limits.

The harsh truth is that someone who remorselessly ignores another's requests when it comes to physical encounters is selfish. If you allow such rude intrusions, be aware that it is not without a high price; your self respect. No matter how alone you may feel, don't allow people to use your body for their own gratification. Such individuals will simply take what they desire, then toss what's left aside like so much chattel.

Carefully ponder the phrase "garbage in, garbage out." The Sacred self is not trash, and should never accept being treated as anything less than a Divine creature.

The Alternative Sexuality
"Spirits, when they please, can assume either sex or both."
— John Milton

There is a whole world, often foreign to those who consider themselves heterosexuals. This is the world of homosexuality, bisexuality, transvestites, and cross-dressers.

In a contemporary setting, people dance around these topics gingerly, like eggs too frail to be broken. But we are adults who have to recognize that Sacredness has many forms of expression. For some people this construct is an alternative life style that deserves respect.

One could conjecture that the cause of such changes developed from a need to be different. We also might wonder if the need to integrate the other half of the yin-yang$_4$ balance effected this movement. Any number of hypotheses could be presented, but theory does not really touch the heart of an individual. Nor will theory tell you how to cope with your own feelings about this subject.

In talking to friends who are both in and out of the proverbial closet, almost all of them still grapple occasionally with guilt feelings created by a non-tolerant society. They are angry, and rightly so, that they are not allowed to love freely without ridicule; that they can not (in most states) legalize their commitment to each other; that they can not openly express their vision of the Sacred Self.

Friends and family may try to be supportive, to understand, but they have not walked a mile in those shoes. Sometimes a father or mother blames themselves for "failing" a child. Sometimes a friend or relative rejects them altogether due to religious conflict. The end result is a muddle of emotional turmoil for everyone involved.

In these moments, return to a very simple school of thought: "people are people." What someone does in private has no effect on how good a friend or co-worker they make. It does not change the things about them you have enjoyed all along. If someone trusts you with this very personal part of their life, you should feel honored. Individuals of alternative sexualities risk much each time they express their lifestyle, not the least of which is possibly loosing intimacy from someone who does not understand.

Personal Diary — August 1985

"I remember working at a summer camp when I was in high school. There was this gorgeous counselor there, who made me laugh and feel so full of life. You can imagine my disappointment to discover he was gay. At first I struggled with this knowledge; after all Christianity is not overly understanding on this issue. Yet the more I knew him, the more I wanted to hold that friendship close to myself. He was someone really special.

Now, over ten years later, I know I made a very good decision. This same wonderful man who took me to my prom when this gawky girl couldn't get a date, flew all the way from LA to be at my wedding. Some friendships, it seems, can traverse far more than miles . . . they also teach you an awful lot about what's really important."

The Other Side of the Soul (Exercise 7)

Each of us has characteristics that are both male or female by design. This is not a sexist comment. From the beginning of time, the basic energy of the universe was divided along these lines. Real power and transformation comes when we recognize and integrate the both polarities as part of a greater whole. This is where transvestites have an advantage. They have lived in both realities, and have an intimate understanding of all the advantages and disadvantages to each.

For this activity find one set of clothing appropriate to the sex opposite from yourself. If possible, include a hat and wig so the transformation is complete as possible. Slowly, as you don this costume, likewise take on a different demeanor. If female, lower your voice by breathing steadily and relaxing your vocal cords, for example. Choose a name for this other side of yourself. Consider what attributes s/he will have, then spend ONE WHOLE DAY in this persona.

This activity works better if you go dressed to a town or city where you're a stranger. That way friends won't recognize Mary who is now Hank, and completely ruin the effect of the persona. Watch closely at how people's reactions to you differ, what kinds of expectations they have for you, and how much control they afford you in various circumstances. If possible, even use the correct bathroom to the situation. For women this presents a small problem with urination, but generally men's lavatories also have "sit down" areas.

The reason for going to this extreme is simple. You can not understand the opposite sex very well since you are not living as that sex. Likewise, you can not always comfortably recognize the attributes of that gender within yourself. One day will not answer all your questions and confusions, but it will help you discover greater balance.

Remember that the soul is non-gender specific. Most people believe that we incarnate, as both sexes at least once to learn more universal lessons. Individuals who take alternative sexual lifestyles may somehow gain that instruction in one life instead of two! This exercise gives you one means to try the "road not taken" for a day and hopefully gain a little insight.

Communicating in Truth & Love (Exercise 8)

Most people know at least one person who is living an

alternative life style. Did you every take the time to talk to them about it? To ask questions and try to understand things from their perspective? If not, then find the time to do just that.

Obviously, it is best if you know this individual fairly well so that your questions will seem intrusive. If you don't have anyone you know that intimately, try contacting a local representative for gay and lesbian awareness organizations. They will be very happy to clear up any misconceptions or apprehensions you may have.

When you go to meet with your resource person, take along a list of all the questions you've always wondered about. Don't feel embarrassed. It is far better to get your information from an informed source than to be mislead by conservative propaganda or even your own uncertainties. You will come away from the experience far more apprized of the realities.

If you feel very awkward about face-to-face interactions, at least call or write and ask for some pamphlets. Part of caring for the Sacred Self comes in the form of education and awareness. The extra time and effort you spend learning about the marvelous diversity of human nature, the more you can appreciate that variety, and yourself as part of that diversity.

Summary

Psychologists and Sociologists agree that liberal societies breed confusion about mores. Every day we are bombarded with opinions on what is best, most beautiful, most enduring, most sensual. Yet these images don't seem to reach us where we live, and rarely reflect the ideal Sacred Self.

Perhaps people around the turn of the century had the

right idea when they espoused nature as the most lovely, perfect reflection of the Divine. Trees do not strive to be like each other. If one is an oak, and another an elm, there is no confusion, no conflict, only calm acceptance. Similarly, rabbits do not strive to outperform each other, and squirrels don't kill each other if one acquires another mate. Each living thing simply moves along their own route to destiny. We could learn much from this world.

Uncovering a peaceful resolve of who we are, what makes us happy, how we can be fulfilled on all levels, is our ultimate goal. Partially realized by knowing that sex is a sacred act and that our bodies are our own property, this is a life-long achievement. Do not be afraid to take control of your physicality, your desires and recognize them as part of yourself and the Divine. When the time is right, reach out to and share the Sacred Self, knowing it is not the act, but the beauty released from within, that makes a moment something truly memorable.

Notes

1. The best explanation I can give of Ky is a kind of sixth sense, an attunement allowing for precise action or inaction. It is an important element to martial arts practices, whose development helps improve self control and alertness.

2. Throughout the body there are energy centers called Chakras. The one near the navel, or just below, is the most important to the concept of centering. This is where most individuals carry their center of gravity.

    Spiritual centering is a means to focus on that singular point, bringing our mind, body and soul back into an equilibrium. One good method is visualizing concentric circles of light moving toward you and into that spot. There, they settle like an anchor, revitalizing energy and harmony.

3. Longer visualizations like this are sometimes easier to use effectively if put on a tape recording before hand. If your own voice distracts you too much, try that of a close friend or mate. These kinds of activities also function with partners or in small group settings, with discussions of success, failure and general feedback afterwards.

4. Yin and Yang in Oriental cultures depict the most perfect, balanced masculine-feminine potency. The circular symbol used to represent them has a black half and a white half, each of which has small central segments of

the other color. This illustrates the idea that one sexuality is never wholly separate from attributes of the other, and the power in their unity.

5. Reincarnation is a very old ideology based on the belief that our soul, the thing which makes us wholly unique, is immutable. Just as energy can not be created or destroyed, the spirit of a person simply changes form upon death.

Some cultures so revere this philosophy that they do not condone killing insects for fear of upsetting karmic balance, or interfering with a soul's chosen journey.

Eight:
Internalizing the Spirit of Beauty
(Rituals for Self-Transformation)

"My art is the painting of soul,
so fine, so exacting, so strange;
To blend in one tangible whole
The manifold features of change."
— Gamaliel Bradford

"Never esteem anything as of advantage to thee that shall
make thee break thy word or loose thy self respect."
— MarcusAurelius

The term "ritual" carries connotations that make some people uncomfortable. Somehow it engenders images of long, dull church services alongside memories of Aunt Martha's chastisement to sit still. For this book, however, ritual has very little to do with that kind of atmosphere. While the efforts you make toward sacred beauty deserve no less reverence, now it is just you and the Divine — no one criticizing you, and no one telling you to do it differently.

By definition, a ritual is anything practiced regularly with some specific order. In this sense, going to work, chewing your food a set number of times, and even cooking dinner have ritualistic aspects. Humans are creatures of habit. We like having some structure to our daily activities.

Mini-rituals of a very simple nature, like the Saturday night bath, developed as one way to identify future events with certainty. Since tomorrow was always somewhat hidden, this afforded peace of mind, like being able to declare with assurance that the grass is, indeed, green. Alongside domestic rites, other religious ones also evolved, giving form and pattern to the Divine and the universe.

Some rituals, specifically those of hearth and home, or those that venerate the Gods are often performed repeatedly. Therefore, as you read the rituals that follow, you should not constrain yourself to only trying them once. Even the marriage rite could be performed again on an anniversary to renew and revitalize that special bond.

Just like learning to remember to brush your teeth as a child, repetition reinforces a specific concept. In this case, rituals reinforce the fact that the Sacred Self is being reborn daily within you. The old aphorism, "you are what you eat," has very strong bearings on this journey towards transformation. We do not simply have to accept all the sociologically-trained garbage we've been fed by the media, our society, the government and even our own kin. The idea behind these rituals is to eventually define your own sense of truth, discover your own image of beauty, then live as that new person in a vibrant, day-to-day reality.

In writing these exercises, I have fallen back on the patterns given to us by teachers of meditation, visualization and various world faiths as a guide. If you are uncomfortable with the wording, approach or any part of an activity, I must stress again that you should follow that voice. Without personal accord and comprehension, any ceremony becomes as meaningless as the rote catechisms of your youth. Make whatever changes you deem necessary so the movements and feelings behind your rituals are of one mind and one soul.

For Improved Self Images
"Self reverence, self knowledge, self control, these three alone lead life to sovereign power. "
— A. Lord Tennyson

Throughout this text, you have defined and delineated your Sacred Self. Unfortunately, life is not always kind or picture perfect. Waves of problems, sorrows and disappointments come to us, wearing away portions of that strong foundation. When such instances occur, it is not a moment for self-chastisement. Just like the old adage about falling off a horse, momentary setbacks in the journey towards self actualization should be just that; momentary. This ritual is created to help to put the saddle of control back on your life, and reaffirm the positive self image you worked so hard to achieve.

Tools Needed: A current picture of yourself, a list of your most positive attributes (in your mind), a brand new outfit (expensive, if possible), a crown of flowers.

Timing: Dawn is the best time of day for this activity. The transformation from shadow to light is very empowering.

Activity: Go somewhere private, preferably outdoors. Sit down for a while before you begin, looking over the aforementioned list and picture closely. Really focus on the spiritual loveliness you radiate even through a photograph.

Remind yourself of how long and hard you have worked toward wholeness. Determine, here and now, that the winds of change will not blow away your resolve. During this time, it is also nice to whisper a brief prayer to welcome an appropriate Divine presence. Whether you're at home or in the woods, the Divine is also there, but will not encroach on your life or sacred space without supplication.

Next, put on the new clothing you brought. As you remove the old clothing, allow each piece to represent a part of your anger, sadness, or other feelings that impede growth. Wrap these clothes in a bundle, but pay no attention to them for the rest of the ritual. They are no longer part of you — disengage those feelings and problems.

The reason I suggest a slightly expensive outfit is that we often hesitate to treat ourselves royally. Donning such attire acts like a coronation rite where you re-accept the rulership of your own life. Lastly, as the first rays of dawn reach the horizon, place the natural crown upon your head; this is where the ancients believed the seat of god abided.

Now, proudly speak your name to the winds. Reach your arms out to the new day and welcome its golden strength. Shout your intentions to every leaf and bud. Phrases such as "I am the ruler of my life and it will be happy," "I accept my God/self as the ultimate leader of my heart — I will trust my instincts," or "I am with God, God is with me, and together we are strong," are all good examples. Sing and dance until you can expend no more energy. Release the power of your sacredness to the world, then sit and relax, letting the winds return those echoes like a gentle blessing. Remember to mark your feelings and observations in your journal.

For Discovering Elemental, Animal and Herbage Personas
"I am the Poem of Earth"
— Walt Whitman

How often have you heard people described as being flowery, agile as cats, faithful as dogs or whimsical as the winds? It is very common to use natural examples when portraying personalities. Is there more to this way of communicating than just simple description? I think so.

Each one of us has certain personality traits mirrored in the natural world. By recognizing those aspects and studying our counterparts we can learn much about ourselves, each other, and the difficulties in human interactions. Say you meet someone and you feel uneasy for no apparent reason. This could indicate deception on their part, or it could indicate a natural energy that is contrary to, or causes static with, your own.

Fiery people, for example, who have lots of overt energy, enthusiasm and will power, get riled up by Air people (fanning the flame). They also might be nervous around water people who, by their calm demeanor, threaten to put those sparks out altogether! Understanding these basic personality types will help you understand your own reactions.

There are many ways to discern personality archetypes, one of the best being simple observations. How does that individual move? How are they built (tall like a tree, with good roots)? Of what does their laugh remind you? How do they react under pressure? With this data in hand, you can almost always find a natural object, animal or element that corresponds. For example, someone with a bird-like persona might also be a nervous nibbler whose easily startled, but has a broad perspective.

Take what you distinguish as being the key component to their personality and put it to practical use for personal and interpersonal transformation. In the aforementioned example,

171

focus on being more aware of your jittery tendencies to calm them, thus making everyone around you more at ease. Also make the most of your unique outlook, offering it in difficult situations.

Here's one ritual for discovering your own archetypal self. It may also be employed for people with whom you interact regularly by changing your center of awareness to one of those individuals. In this instance, however, please take care not to perform the rite out of random curiosity. Just as your innermost nature is very private, discernment of others must be done with reverence for their privacy, and only when there is a real need:

Tools Needed: Books with pictures of animals, elements and flowers/trees. If possible some music with natural sounds (such as a waterfall or crickets).

Timing: Whatever time of day you feel sharpest, most alive and aware.

Activity: Again insure yourself of some private time. Try not to have any expectations on what you may see, hear, smell or even taste during this meditation. While you relax, take a few moments to skim the pages of the magazines or books you brought. Do not focus on any one section too long or it could predispose your subconscious. Just browse casually, then set the books aside for research later.

Get comfortable, welcome your protective, guiding God/dess and visualize yourself as you sit right now. See every curve, every taught muscle, every shade of color. Breath deeply in self awareness. Notice your unique body scent. Listen to the music of your heart and breathing. Feel the texture of your aura in the air.

Slowly, allow this image to become fuzzy around the edges, like hazy light that's not totally in focus. Allow this light to swirl and move like clouds in your mind's eye. Watch closely for images that form or appear in the haze. At first, you are likely to see predominant situations that lay heavy on your heart. As you do, release them and the image should shift again.

Once the hurried portraits of current concerns slow or stop completely, ask your guide or higher self for the most complete symbolic representation of yourself. The words, "Let me see myself in total truth" are very powerful at this juncture. Then wait calmly until the clouds of spirit begin to shape themselves again.

In this ritual, many people will discover the face of an animal with whom they have always shared a special rapport, the image of a plant whose scent uplifts them, or even an element in which they have always felt more alive (like being energized by a waterfall). This is not surprising. Most of us have some rudimentary awareness of this central nature, it's just that we never had a way of putting it into words.

For those who see something completely surprising, try and discover the lessons to learn there. Our deepest natures are sometimes hidden from us because of memories, fears, self doubts and confusions. When it appears for the first time, we can be startled by the wonder of it. Don't be afraid to look at a genuine, legitimate representation of your Sacred Self. The more you know, and the more you perceive with wisdom, the more you become an participant in your own transformation.

Make notes of your discovery in your journal, and

research the various habits, folklore, and superstitions for what you have seen. By so doing, the person who sees themselves as a daisy, for example, discovers that this flower always turns to follow the light of the sun, meaning their path is moving in the right direction. The person who discovers themselves as a fox might realize this vision reminds them of their ability to move shrewdly and unobtrusively through difficult situations.

It should be noted that after drastic life experiences the procedure should be repeated to see if anything has changed. Very frequently the image you receive will vary, reflecting the modifications going on within; the new person you have become because of those experiences. This visage may help to explain feelings you have been struggling with, or grant renewed confidence through knowing that transformation is, indeed, occurring.

For Emotional Healing (Personal)

"Success is not determined by what life hands you, but what you hand life in return."
— Marian LoreSinger

Life rarely deals out the set of cards for which we most hope; perfect health, perfect love, perfect peace. There are many scenarios that require some type of healing slave for the emotional wounds received. If this healing doesn't occur our heart can close, and we find ourselves hiding in a kind of unfeeling pantomime that is really only pretense. This pantomime hinders the developing Sacred Self on fundamental levels.

So what's the cure? First and foremost, start by eliminating phrases like "stupid mistakes", and "stupid questions" from your vocabulary. There is no such thing unless you learn nothing from the experience.

Secondly, realize that although you are partially Divine, none of us has reached Godhood yet. So, mistakes, problems, anguish and recuperation are just one more part of that human equation. Despite appearances, we are never totally alone in our problems. Somewhere, someone like us is going through much the same thing, and feels just as alone. Knowing this is the first step toward recovery.

Tools: A bed, a candle, incense which has either cinnamon, mint, bay or thyme in it (for psychic awareness), spring water in a basin with rose petals.

Timing: The night, darkness, when sorrow can emerge freely. Just before bed time.

Activity: If physical restrictions allow, this rite is more effective if you can fast the day before. This purges your body of toxins similarly to those pains you wish to purge from your heart.

The purpose of this activity is inspiring what I call guided dreaming where you are an active participant in your own healing, as well as that of another person. To begin, wash your forehead (the area of psychic impressions known as the third eye) with the rose water. This is for cleansing and self love. Next, light your candle and some incense, saying a brief prayer to your chosen Guardian Spirit.

Sit on the edge of the bed, looking towards the candle.

Breath deeply and begin to recount the circumstances that caused distress and the need for healing. Allow all the emotions you kept to yourself to surface. Hold yourself tightly, cry, rock, pace the floor, yell if it helps, but don't hold back.

When you feel empty, turn your attention back to the candle. Feel its warmth calming your nerves and entering your soul. Slowly as you observe the dancing flame, breath out your negative emotions on one huge gulp of air and extinguish the light from the room. Lie down, continuing to maintain a meditative state. See yourself as you are now, with your arms outstretched as if to give or receive a hug. Send love and warmth through your fingertips, like red beams, to someone in the universe who feels as you do. Release the energy, then see other similar rays of radiant warmth returning to your heart. Let them wrap around like a cocoon of love until you fall into peaceful slumber.

At this point you may or may not dream. Most people report having very vivid, often inspirational dreams that help them regain composure and confidence. Exactly what happens to you will be completely unique and focused on your situation.

In my own experience after this meditation, I felt lifted from my body and transported somewhere else. There before me I saw a young girl weeping. She was angry and hurt because her ideas were far beyond that of the traditional world in which she lived. She had dared to dream! Suddenly she turned her head, somewhat startled, but seemed to sense that someone was there. I reached a hand out to stroke her head and spoke only four words, "you are not alone." In that moment sorrow fell from her face like a curtain to the floor, replaced with the most calm, comforted smile. I could not help but smile too. In our moment of shared frustration, two souls embraced outside of time and renewed each other's hope.

For Improved Balance and Centering
"Poetic Justice, with her lifted scale, Where in nice balance truth with gold, she weighs. "
— Alexander Pope

A number of situations on the Path of Beauty call for tremendous amounts of grace and poise under pressure. Moments when friends and family depend on us for strength and assurance; moments when we must depend on ourselves for fortitude; moments amidst the clamor of life that leave us feeling totally perplexed.

Taking a deep breath and stopping to think before we act can help tremendously. Nonetheless, this may not be sufficient for composed logical thought. So, when a moment avails itself, try this meditation/visualization for bringing everything back to an even keel. The purpose of this ritual is to develop enough personal equilibrium to deal with the situation more effectively.

Tools: A private space, a circular object or picture of concentric circles that you can easily remember and imagine. Two candles.

Timing: Noon or Midnight, Dawn and Sunset when time and light both hang in the balance.

Activity: As with the other exercises in this book, take a few moments to calm your nerves. Sit quietly in the center of a rug or floor, breathing in a slow, rhythmic, connected manner. As you do, take time to focus your attention on the circular object or concentric circles until a clear image of this can be seen in your mind's eye.

Next, light one of the two candles, placing it nearest your weaker hand. The unlit candle goes on the opposite side of your body near the hand with which you write. Make sure these are a safe distance away from your body and properly contained as your eyes will be closed.

Now, close your eyes. Continue breathing in through your nose, out through your mouth, feeling the energy and warmth of each breath. This is vital, life-giving power that carries rejuvenation to each cell. Slowly allow the remaining tensions to fall away from you with every breath, pushing the frustrations and anger away with your personal wind of change.

Next, focus your attention on the candles beside you, not with your physical eyes, but your senses. Notice the warmth of one, the cool potential in the other. The light of the first brings strength to your weaknesses, the dark of the second brings peace to your active mind. Feel yourself between the two, and slowly bring that energy into balance.

Finally, reach your hands slowly towards the sky, keeping them an equal distance apart so that they do not disrupt this balance. Envision the sphere or circles you studied before descending on to your hands, then slipping over your body, slowly anchoring themselves near your navel. This area is a mooring for your emotional storm, your center of power. Remember where the spheres settle in the hours and days ahead so that you can breath from that region, taking up the fortitude placed there for reinforcement. Repeat any time you need extra security.

For Marriage and Conception Rites

"Love is not hot-house flower, but a wild plant born of a wet night, born of an hour of sunshine, born of a wild seed, blown along the roads by a wild wind."

— John Galsworthy

Marriage and conception rituals share much in common. Both offer a strong unity of Yin and Yang, both are enacted in love and trust, both are tremendous commitments, and both mark the beginning of a new creature — either the spiritually united couple or a soul. In addition, many of the symbols used for these ceremonies can be the same; roses for love, yellow decorations for creativity, the image of a pregnant goddess to bring fruitfulness and joy, and the exchange of tokens to mark the occasion.

On the Path of Beauty, these moments denote a change from a singular quest to one where we share the road with another. This change can be a shock to anyone who has never adjusted their reality for the sake of another. As such, marriage (or long-term live-ins) and birth are perhaps two of the most growth-oriented experiences in one's life.

The ritual presented here is for a private rite between a couple. It should take place before either the marriage or the attempt to conceive (including before placing adoption papers or artificial insemination). Since these occasions are terribly personal in nature, you may find you have to drastically change this approach to suit your situation. Take some time before hand to talk this over with significant others and decide how to best proceed.

Tools: Two white candles, a bowl of rose petals, one yellow candle, tokens to exchange, possibly a love potion (see Chapter 5).

Timing: For the conception ritual, it is best to try during the woman's natural ovulation cycle. For marriage, any personally significant date. Additionally, both are considered more advantageous during a waxing to full moon.

Activity: The couple should come together in total nakedness.

On the floor (or around the bed) a circle of roses can be sprinkled to surround you with loving, tender energies. On a table nearby, have two white candles burning with the yellow one in the center unlit. If a love or fertility potion is to be used, have one cup filled with same to show unity of mind and purpose. Tokens can be purely personal such as jewelry for marriage and baby items for conception.

Once the room is set, the couple should sit in a comfortable position across from each other, matching each other's breathing as closely as possible. When they are in unison, each takes their strong hand to the others aura and begins to stroke it, beginning at the heart and moving in circular patterns outward. Please note that this massage never touches the skin at this point. Instead it blends the outward physical energy, most often experienced through body heat, into harmony.

When the entire auric field has been massaged into the

loving atmosphere, speak your intentions to each other. If wishing to have a child, share your feelings with the spirit (already alive or waiting for birth) that lingers on the edge of your life. If for marriage, tell your partner what it is that is so special about them, and your dreams of what you wish to build. Pray together for divine guidance, patience and vision. Then light the yellow candle to welcome the new trinity; the Sacred We or the advent of a child.

Exchange your tokens at this point, explaining why you chose them, then embrace and spend the rest of the time letting nature have Her way. Do not rush from this nest you have gently built, but hold each other in tenderness until it seems "right" to let go and move onward. Extinguish your candles with a silent prayer of thankfulness for your blessings.

*For Improved Sexual Enjoyment

"All who would joy win, must share in it; happiness was born a twin."

— Lord Byron

One of the major discomforts with marriage and conception rituals comes because many people are uncomfortable with nakedness and physical affection. For them, there is still something that equates sex with sin and dirtiness instead of a beautiful natural expression between two loving adults. The lessons of our childhood and teenage years weigh heavy on our adult interactions. Even so, there are techniques that can at least help us break the ice.

Rather than constructing a ritual for this purpose, I designed this section with some pragmatic advise. If this advise falls short, consult a counselor who specializes in sexual inhibitions to achieve the freedom you deserve.

Aid 1 — Massage

Massage, when done correctly, brings relaxation and sexual release. For someone who is already edgy, it is important that the initial stages are very non-threatening (in other words, no where near the genitalia). Begin with soft movements at the temples, brushing or stroking the hair, massaging the neck, shoulders and hands. Work from the extreme outward portions of the body inward, with tremendous sensitivity.

This is not a good activity for someone who has trouble containing their "wandering hands" even when snuggling. If you rush too quickly here, you will disrupt all the good you hoped to achieve. If need be, take a cold shower first so that both you and your partner can "warm up" together toward a mutually satisfying experience.

Aid 2 — Rhythmic Breathing and Auric Massage

As was described in the marriage and conception rites, breathing in unison and auric massage can help a couple become far more attuned to each other. Sex is an act of passion, and passion rarely has forethought or selflessness. By harmonizing, two people become a functional unit before moving into foreplay, thereby increasing pleasure for both.

Most people find the auric or "ghost" massage very invigorating. The energy brushing lightly over the skin heightens awareness and anticipations. Most people need and want to be touched, so this can become a delightful "teasing" game for mutual gratification.

Aid 3 — Healthful Fantasy

There are sexual fantasies that everyone keeps to themselves for a variety of reasons. However, you may discover that sharing those fantasies, and even making them into a visualization for your partner, can help you over some rough spots. In this case, both individuals find common traits among their imaginings, then make up a story that can be envisioned or even played out in the home. Talking about our fantasies, or playing them out within reason, can ignite a fire to warm up relationships growing cold.

*For Healing Others

"Break up the night and make it beautiful"
— Bayard Taylor

How often have you reached out to hold a friend in need and felt like the gesture was less than you wished it? The touch of a caring hand is highly underrated in our materialistic society, and may hold the cure for many ills.

Throughout this text I have spoken about auric massage and touch therapy. Both of these techniques were used on me after a serious automobile accident, affording comfort far beyond what any medication offered. This personal experience, combined with research, leads me to believe that restorative energy is not limited to those called to healing arts. Instead, all of us have potential "healing in our hands!" From this premise, if we add a little creative visualization, our touches can ease the physical and emotional pain of others.

I can not stress enough, however, that a real trust and understanding must exist between two individuals before attempting an effort like this. You are working very intimately with another's energies — and unfortunately, some people can misinterpret your efforts by emotionally or physically latching on. This is quite natural, but very awkward until straightened out.

In instances where the individual in question might not be ready for deeper workings, stick to a gentle hug and allow their pain to flow through you into the floor like a tree moves water and sap. Do not hold on to it; do not focus directly on it — IT IS NOT YOUR PAIN. Let it go.

For people who are closer to you, the following activity should prove very helpful:

Tools: A comfortable place to lie dow that is accessible from all four sides, some oil of frankincense & myrrh, soothing music, dim lighting.

Timing: When the need arises.

Activity: This exercise blends basic massage techniques with auric cleansing and balancing. If your spiritual energy is out of whack, it is all but impossible to get your emotions or physical nature back in sync. If your partner is accustom to meditation, it helps if they put themselves in a receptive state before starting. If not, you may have to talk them through with quiet, guiding words and rich imagery until they reach a dreamy calm.

Begin the music (which should be as inspirational for you as it is for your partner) and anoint your palms with the oil. I have chosen this particular scent because it has long associations with purification, cleansing, protection and sacred rites. Prepare yourself mentally in whatever manner feels suitable — pray, meditate, or begin your breathing exercises to center your mind and heart on becoming an instrument for Divine energy.

As you place your hands above your partner, start on any section which of the body nearest you. About 6" above the skin is a good height to sense auric textures. Take time to survey this entire side of your partner's body. Note any areas in which the aura which feel bumpy, itchy, or just different from the rest. These are the areas where you need to channel energy to reestablish equilibrium.

To do this, envision white-blue sparkling light pouring from above your head, through your arms and out through your palms. You may find that your hands become numb or tingly during this, which is a pretty good sign you're doing it right. Continue in this manner until the entire aura on this side of the body feels aligned.

You can now go ahead with a more physical massage (gentle). When you reach the feet, hands and head, make sure to take a moment to place your own palms on the ground to pour out any residual tension or sickness. Also, take the time to pour some white light energy into each of the energy centers at the top of the head, the third eye, throat, heart, stomach, genital region and feet.

Finally, instruct your partner to roll over from their pelvis SLOWLY. Repeat the same procedure on the other side of the body, instructing your partner to stay and rest until they feel ready to return to normal awareness. Many people feel quite giddy after this experience, and most benefit from it.

Always wash your hands when you are completed and release your partners pains, tensions or sicknesses to the power of water.

For Overcoming Fears and Barriers

"In the darkest night of the year, when the stars have all gone out, that courage is better than fear, that faith is truer than doubt."

— Washington Gladden

There are many situations in life where physical and emotional closeness hinders perspective. This includes fear, and anything perceived as a hindrances. When we expect a problem, or anticipate difficulty, sure enough, one usually greets us!

When I was growing up we fostered a young man in our home. Chris was "hampered" in that he was developmentally disabled by Downs syndrome. Yet, Chris seemed to have no idea that he was supposed to be limited in any way. If we had told him, "you won't be able to do things like 'normal children'" I hate to think what fate might have become this loving youth. He did not accept limitations because, for him, there were none other than those he found in himself.

How often do we become so consumed by fear or overwhelmed by an obstacle that we're unable or unwilling to act? To illustrate, the person who fails an initial road test is not necessarily a bad driver. They may have been too nervous to function properly. However, if they perceive this failure as a prelude to all future attempts, they may give up trying altogether and take the bus instead! A positive personal outlook is the major differentiating factor between those who succeed and those who don't, along with determination.

Toning, chants and mantras are tools that can help retrain your mind to think and act in a more dauntless manner. Practice these daily with your other spiritual pursuits, changing them to directly relate to your needs. Which technique, or which combinations chosen, depend greatly on how comfortable you are with the method(s), and which one(s) best suits your circumstances.

Toning: is considered a singular sound at a distinct pitch that is carried for a length of time, usually that of one complete breath. Most often, toning uses singular consonants or vowels to produce specific results in the body and psyche.

To get the most effect out of toning, sit or stand upright. Think of power building as you inhale, then let energy be released with a singular sound on exhaling. The sound should be carried on the complete, steady and slow exhalation, so that the force fills the room. Sometimes people notice their nose tingles a little during toning, this is a good indication of performing it correctly.

Here are some simple tones to try. The M or Ma sound is maternal and nurturing, especially helpful in healing or finding comfort. O is a lunar sound, full of insight, cycles, and openings. Ah is the vibration of relief and can help reduce stress. N is an active tone, energizing and empowering especially when you need to say "no". Finally, I is the vowel of self, and U is the vowel of awareness towards others.

As a side note, toning can be a powerful tool that focuses harmony among groups. Each person begins with their own inspired tone, and slowly the sound around the gathering likens itself to a spiritual chorus, filled with each individual's sacredness. A cadence and underlying melody will slowly evolve, crescendo, then die down, at which point the group is in proper accord for almost any endeavor.

Chants: Chants may be sung or intoned, but frequently contain more than one word. They are defined best as short prayers or songs with simple, repetitive patterns that encourage a meditative state. By this definition, the rosary might be considered a tool for Christian chanting.

Chants can be those heard frequently at gatherings, those of Native American traditions, or ones of our own devising. Whatever you choose, it should reflect your desire to overcome, be a victor instead of a victim, and become the master of your life. Here is one that is excellent for this particular scenario. Each phrase should be repeated thrice before moving on to the next:

Strength
Strength & Power
Strength, Power and Confidence
Strength, Power, Confidence and Victory
all these things are part of me.

If spoken or sung, the phrases begin in a whisper until the energy naturally encourages your voice to rise to the sky. When you feel the word power has been released to do its work, slowly reduce volume again, then sit quietly in the center of the protective, invigorating vortex you have created.

Mantra: Comes from a Sanskrit word meaning prayer or hymn.

Hindus use these in the belief that a person's mantra embodies their divinity and invokes a special power within. At least part of this word, "man," probably directly relates to the function of the mind or the quality of mind necessary for the discipline. Most people believe the mantra to be a very personal thing, that may or may not be totally understood by the user. For example, when I was meditating one day, certain one and two syllable words kept coming to mind. I wrote them down and shared them with a teacher whom I respected. He suggested they may be a personal mantra, and to try looking up the words in various languages. As it turned out, the words were very meaningful to me and explained much of my Karmic ties to people. I found that repeating the mantra when meditating helped bring peace and centering in a manner that I'd never experienced before.

One of the most successful ways to discover your mantra is to start by intoning the "Om" or "I am." Breath in, then release the word(s) when you exhale. If other phrases or words follow of their own accord, make sure you have a notebook handy and write them down. If they seem to be nonsense, go to your library to check language books.

Once you feel fairly certain that the phrase you have is complete (usually not much more than 7 words), speak it out loud during times of stress. Begin with the first word repeated three times (the number of body-mind-soul), then add to it the next word, again three times. Continue building in this manner until the whole mantra resonates through you like a chord of music, strengthening inner foundations.

Some people believe that the Mantra reflects the best of our accumulated knowledge and wisdom as achieved through the ages. As such, it is a powerful tool in overcoming fears and overcoming any obstacles that attempt to obstruct the Path of Beauty.

Coping with Anger & Loss
*"Cease from anger at the fates which thwart themselves so
madly. Live and learn, not first learn and then live."*
— Robert Browning

Grief and outrage are two of the most difficult emotions
for people to handle constructively. Their depth and breadth
effect the human psyche so powerfully as to rival love. Grief
leaves us with many unanswered questions and regrets.
Outrage often flares out of control, all too frequently hurting
those who don't deserve our ire, or our erratic moods.

In both these instances the first and most important step
is recognizing your emotions for what they are. Grief is a
natural part of a cycle that will pass. In order for it to do so,
you must be willing to let go. Likewise, anger is something
that moves upon us so quickly that we act before thinking.

Once you have worked through your feelings a little, you
can re-approach the situation. Forgiveness of self, of any
others involved, and a willingness to leave this whole situation
behind you are the best allies in the healing process. While we
may not ever forget a loved one who passes over, or
sometimes recall painful arguments long after they're resolved,
too much attention to these negative feelings can bring them
to the surface all over again. Leave the past behind, dwell in
the now, and realize that the Sacred Self waits patiently for
you in the future.

One ritual that I found personally successful in easing
both anger and loss follows. Please try to prepare yourself.
This meditation brings a lot of intense, unexpected emotions
to bear. Experience these feelings fully, then release them to
the earth so healing begins. If possible, have a trusted friend

work with you through the rite, keeping a comforting hand and plenty of tissues at the ready.

Tools: A picture of the individual who was lost or who you were angry towards (in some cases it may be both). A single candle of their favorite color. Any breakable symbols of your negative feelings (including guilt).

Timing: After an argument, as soon as you are truly ready to bring forgiveness to your heart. With loss, I suggest 1-2 months to the date after passing at the latest. If this is not possible, try the one-year anniversary date.

Activity: Create a sacred space in whatever manner is comfortable to you, welcoming your God/dess to grant guidance, protection, perspective and healing energy. Get comfortable, sitting at a table or on the floor within arms reach of the candle. Concentrate all your energy on the picture you have brought. Allow it to become the essence of that person, with all the emotions associated with that name and face.

Next, light the candle and say, "I welcome the spiritual energy of _____ in my sacred space." The individual may or may not respond on an astral level to your call, but at least you have left the door open for their participation. Now close your eyes.

Envision a three dimensional image of that person directly in front of you, holding your hands. Smell their cologne or perfume, see them wearing favorite clothes, make note of all their features. The more vivid this image becomes, the more effective the rite.

Begin to speak to the person, telling them everything you

feel (both good and bad). Be totally honest, but gentle with your words, not only with them but with yourself. Pour out everything on your heart until you feel all the sorrow or anger leave, like a glass being emptied. At this point you may sense that the image before you has a message in return. If so, carefully heed their words, noting them in your journal for future consideration.

Finally, release that person from your expectations, and release yourself from grief and anger. Say out loud: "I free you and I free myself; our pathway together is whole again. The past is behind us. We walk now, each in their own way, towards whatever the future holds."

In your minds eye, release the hands of your specter and see the two of you doing one of two things. For grief, it is best to envision the person walking away from you over a bridge towards a beautiful white light. The bridge is the binding tie of life. Know they are at peace. For anger, it might be better to see the two of you walking over a bridge together. In this case the movement represents moving away from harsh feelings towards peace and reconciliation.

Once you complete this exercise, continue doing whatever it takes to settle matters in your mind and heart, specifically making an apology or opening the door for reconciliation in the case of anger. For loss, the best medicine is time and moving onward. Those who have loved you only want the best for you, so go forward on the Path of Beauty, knowing in some small way, that spirit walks with you.

*For Encouraging One World Perspectives

"Behold how good and how pleasant it is for brethren to dwell together in unity."

Psalms CXXXIII.I

Slowly, our yearning for the Sacred Self extends its boundaries. Our new awareness reminds us that we are not alone on this Earth; thousands of souls are in this classroom together. Around the world, every day, people strive for the same sense of spirituality for which you have fought. This commonality of desire creates positive energy that can act as a healing salve to the spirit of Gaia.

The Earth as our Mother can not help but somehow reflect the state of her children. She too is frustrated, trying to find ways to fight back, to reclaim her sacredness and sanctity. Over thousands of years, the human animal has slowly sectionalized both her lands and her babies from one another — tearing them asunder and turning their goals away from Universal good. Now that you are moving towards a more Divine outlook, it is a good opportunity to reverse this separatist ideology.

Tools: A picture of earth from space and several images of a wide diversity of cultural groups in customary attire. A huggable earth pillow or ball (or anything round which can symbolize it).

Timing: Earth Day, during times of social upheaval in specific regions, during peace talks.

Activity: Take an hour or so to review the images you have brought so that you can recall them clearly with your eyes closed. As you do, consider your own desires for world peace and equality, an end to pollution and other ills that ravage the planet. Allow those desires to build within you until you feel ready to burst.

Next, get yourself into a meditative state of mind in whatever manner you choose. When you feel calm and centered, see the world as it moves in space, warmed and brought to life by the vibrant sun. Sense the vitality of the world you observe, how it is a living thing that sustains us all. Slowly, around this image add the faces of the cultural groups, one at a time, each extending a welcoming hand to the other until the Earth is surrounded by a common goal of peace and love.

Now, add your hand to theirs, giving the Earth a huge hug, releasing into the image all the positive energy you built up earlier in the exercise. When you are finished, go out and appreciate a little bit of nature. Clean up your block, collect some recyclables, or whatever. Match your ritual's intentions with physical energy to enhance it every day of your life.

*For Communing with Universal Energy
"That minister of ministers, Imagination, gathers up the undiscovered Universe, like jewels in a jasper cup."
— John Davidson

Spiritual growth often requires a deeper understanding of what are considered "mysteries." The universe is full of pulse and rhythm, unwritten truths and myriads of symbols that await our discovery. When one of these small wonders unfolds, it becomes a sprouting seed in the garden of a self actualized soul, and one less roadblock along the Path of Beauty.

This visualization brings you into closer union with that celestial music, or the Music of the Spheres as Pythagoras called it. This great philosopher expounded on a universal canticle as being an integral part of what held everything in balance. Once discovered, he believed it could help mankind unravel the enigmas of all time. Now you can discover this song as your very own.

Tools: A picture of a spiral galaxy (in color) and some planetarium type music. A handful of glitter.

Timing: Outside (if possible) at night, when the stars are in their glory.

Activity: Once you have found a spot where at least a few stars are visible (in the city rooftops sometimes afford this vantage point), go out before it gets really dark and watch as the night mariners appear one by one. With each new light appearing, release a little tension from the day; release yourself from rushing. You are now in a place that is timeless; where forever is now.

When the sky is completely dark, hold your handful of glitter to your heart, and dare to wish upon it. See yourself in every grain of that dust, then release it to the sky to join the stars. As soon as you hand opens, close your eyes and feel the small twinkling specks travel towards the farthest depths of space. Past the moon, past the nearest star, taking you farther and farther into the center of the universe.

As you travel, allow the image of the galaxy you brought

with you to appear just ahead on your journey. As you get closer, you notice it seems to pulse and sing, drawing you into its core. Closer still -- in the nucleus of the galaxy you see a heart, beating, nourishing, pounding for all humankind to hear. Listen closely to that heartbeat, and know it to be your own. You are now one with that heart, that song. The glitter has embedded itself in the center of the galaxy and exploded into bountiful light that is warm, radiating, and part of you. Rest here a while before traveling home, noting your feelings. Make sure to write these observations in your journal after the ritual.

* * *

This chapter has illustrated but a few exercises that reinforce sacred beauty for the self, others and the world. These activities can be performed any time you feel the need. No matter what else, however, please remember that life itself is a ritual, an act of worship, that accentuates the Sacred Self if you let it. It does not take a guru to make life something truly special.

Every moment of every day is an opportunity to better yourself or the lives of others. From the simplest gesture to the greatest extension of love, we have the power within us to bring about transformation. Never give up this desire; never stop believing you are not worth the fight. In the greater scheme of things each atom is important, each moment a miracle, each dream a song, and every person a small fraction of the Great Spirit.

Nine:
The Butterfly of The Soul

The beauty of a butterfly's wing, the beauty of all things
is not a slave to purpose, a drudge sold to futurity.
It is excrescence, superabundance, random ebullience"
— Donald C. Peattie

"We may well adorn and beautify, in scrupulous self
respect, our souls, and whatever our souls touch upon."
— Walter Pater

In ancient civilizations, philosophers likened the butterfly to the human soul's journey of transformation. As with any creature of loveliness, it was assigned significance among benevolent spirits or symbols, namely that of metamorphosis. Its birth as one creature, then temporary "death" and rebirth to a new, more beautiful existence became the perfect representation of reincarnation. Additionally, these three stages closely resemble the degrees of many mystery schools; that of neophyte, intermediary, and finally the adept who is free to fly away from the baser human nature.

In your quest for the Sacred Self, I can predict with 100% accuracy that you will encounter at least one stumbling block that seems unsurmountable. In facing these barriers, remember that quality learning is rarely instantaneous. This blockade becomes a time of waiting; of gestation, like a tutoring cocoon.

Consider for a moment that the caterpillar is a rather ugly, insignificant insect with little of interest to hold one's attention. Some are gawky, some rotund, some are fuzzy and some are bald. Yet these creatures eventually break free from this external mirage and take on exquisite beauty. In the initial stages of reclaiming personal sanctity, you become this caterpillar. As you nibble on the first green sprouts of self confidence, the energy of transformation grows in your heart. This transformation cannot be rushed, but gently follows nature's pathway.

In the process of growing, likewise remember that the butterfly did not always have wings. In our urgent desire to re-establish the Sacred Self, we may hasten across some barriers without proper preparation, without maturity as a guide. Or, maybe the barrier itself is an instructor. The old saying "walls can talk" has some real validity here. What's yours trying to tell you?

This chapter offers a few more ideas on how to handle those frustrating moments. Above all else, please don't give up and forego the ancient powers altogether. If you relinquish the quest for sacredness now, you may never take the bold step to try again later. Dare to dream.

The Caterpillar
"It is easy to be brave from a safe distance"

— Aesop

The Caterpillar is the child within each of us. This spirit is uncertain, vulnerable, and somewhat blind. When we first embark on the quest toward wholeness, we have little idea of what we're going to encounter or achieve. We feel curious, frightened and anxious all at once. Our spiritual hunger gnaws within, urging us to seek out the right nourishment for the soul.

The caterpillar stage is basically one of examination and experimentation. Life now become a subject for inspection and pondering. At first this whole review can seem daunting — rather like the caterpillar looking up a huge stalk to see its supper at the top!

At some point that obstacle has to be surmounted, but at first it looks too damn big; too frightening; like too much of a commitment. So instead of rushing head-on, explore your options a bit. You may discover, like our allegorical friend, that you have a far greater capacity to overcome the insurmountable than you ever thought.

This is what I call the "Ah, Ha!" syndrome. All at once a light goes on, and the window of opportunity slides open. You can literally see when this happens to someone. His or her face becomes bright, their eyes twinkle, and their next action takes place naturally with real determination. Somehow this person has finally found a source of nourishment from which to feed the Sacred Self — and nothing should stand in their way of getting to that source.

Folklore, Superstition & The Sacred Self
"It is the customary fate of new truths to begin as heresies and to end as superstitions."
— Thomas H. Huxley

In the wild, caterpillars eat what most humans consider a simple weed to grow to their full size and prepare for the cocoon stage. For humans, this translates into falling back on commonly known things; simple ideas that we can digest easily. Myths, fables from our youth, and proverbs are just such spiritual foods.

By now you have probably noticed that throughout this text I used aphorisms, lore or common folk beliefs as part of visualizations or other exercises. Many of these adages have been around for hundreds, if not thousands, of years. Any idea held in collective belief systems long enough takes on a life and power all its own. Then too, since folkways originated from the best teacher known, that of observation, many of them have some level of scientific validity.

With or without that extra bit of documentation, all of us have grown up with sayings that we remember and follow routinely. Do you walk under or around ladders? Toss spilled salt over your shoulder? Wash your windows when you want it to rain? The ritualistic nature of aphorisms gives them unseen potential, which the creative spiritual seeker may tap.

This section is included to offer you one more possible, familiar tool in your journey toward self transformation. Whether you try some of the examples given herein or create some of your own, I think you will find wive's tales can really make a difference toward fulfilling your spiritual appetite when you've reached an impasse. After all, if it takes a bit of superstition to warrant definitive action founded in self confidence, then I am more than happy to rank myself among the superstitious!

Luck

Luck is an uncomfortable word to many of us, being linked to chance and fate. Yet in reflecting upon, and reclaiming the Sacred Self, luck is certainly something of which we could all use a little extra. During those times when you feel as if good fortune has disappeared, try performing all your regular morning functions moving from the right side first. In other words, get up on the "right foot."

Pass all your food and drink at the table in the direction of the sun's natural movement. This encourages both luck and health. Within your home, consider keeping some Holly, Laurel or Elder to protect you from unwanted negative energies. Finally, sweep your ill fortune out the door with a handy kitchen broom!

Prosperity

Money certainly can't buy happiness, but having enough to care for ourselves and our loved ones is very important to overall self esteem. To this end, folklore tells us to keep rice, bread or corn in the house as symbols of Nature's bounty. Left over bread should never be thrown away — that tosses out your fortune. Instead, share it with the birds and give back to Gaia a bit of her blessings.

Another way to increase funds is to go outside on the night of a new moon and turn a silver coin over in your pocket. Alternatively, turn your purse. The rotating motion is said to "turn" prosperity in your direction. Afterwards, be sure to make a real effort to aid this kind of sympathetic magic along. Basically, don't ask the universe for money then sit home instead of looking for a job. The universe meets our attempts at least half way, but half of zero is still zero!

Relationships

Our search for wholeness becomes even more evident during those times when we look to share ourselves with others. Many people feel inadequate in their interpersonal relationships, as if they are not worthy of love. Our ancestors understood these feelings as intimately as we do, and often sought refuge and security in the little sayings learned at the feet of their parents. We continue to see many of these superstitions at weddings today, with "old, new, borrowed, and blue" being the most widely known. Here are two others for you to consider:

* Commitments in relationships are best done during the waxing to full moon, so that love and caring can grow to their fullness.
* A bundle of coriander hung in your home brings harmony to all within. Find some fresh at a market and think agreeable thoughts each time you look upon the packet.

Natural Connections

If one of your spiritual goals is coming into closer harmony with nature, then folklore has marvelous avenues to explore. For example, moonlit nights among the wildflowers, specifically foxglove and thyme, is the best time to see fairies. Using the same reasoning, it may also be the best interval for meditations to contact the $devic_1$ realms.

Health

How we feel daily effects our self image. It's hard to project the image of strength, confidence and assurance when you have a runny nose! While folklore may not cure your malady, it does have several "charms"$_2$ to safeguarded your health. Some of these may have actual value since doctors who carried aromatic herbs, and those who worked in perfumeries during plagues evidenced a significantly lower incident of contagion. These herbs included rosemary, clover and myrtle to ward sickness, and lily of the valley, lavender and mint to ease depression. Try making a little cache for yourself and carrying it in a brief case or purse to transport the energy of well being with you everywhere.

The Cocoon
"Closed and safe within its central heart, nestles the seed perfection."
— Walt Whitman

At some point in the caterpillars journey, it finds it can eat no more. It is weary and quite ready to burst away from the old constraining mold. So, it weaves a protective cocoon around itself where it can slowly meet destiny face to face.

For some individuals this cocoon takes the form of a sanctuary, a place where they feel totally safe and protected. For others it is a time of retreat. If you watch the caterpillar as it weaves a cocoon, you will notice that the strands are carefully laid to protect and nurture. Within this darkened shell, they are totally alone.

On the Path of Beauty, the cocoon is a time of true introspection, where we can grapple with our own darkness. Like Moses in the wilderness, much can be said for those moments when there's nothing between us and the Gods but the sky and our faith.

Weaving the Cocoon (Exercise 1)
The cocoon is a place of rest and solitude. It can be a physical place or a secret hideaway in your own mind and

heart. During times of tremendous transitions, sometimes we need to weave the cocoon for protection, warmth and a sense of solidarity unknown in the open world. This action should not be mistaken for hiding. It is instead a preparation to accept all that comes with change.

During those times when you feel a tremendous need or urge to be totally alone, find a way to answer the call of your spirit. Go to the woods, rent a hotel room, or arrange a day by yourself. Once solitude has been achieved, try this visualization to emphasize your soul-searching:

Get into a comfortable position. Draw the drapes and wait until nightfall. Return to a meditative state of mind. For some people this exercise is more effective if they curl up in a fetal position; the natural shape of human growth and birth. This posture can be difficult to maintain throughout the exercise, however, so judge according to your own physical needs.

Next, envision yourself taking strands of silver-white thread from your chakras, and laying them carefully around yourself starting beneath your feet. Slowly watch as the cocoon builds. Sense the transitional energy and strength of the weaving. Continue to place the strands around until you are enclosed completely. This is your cave of mysteries, a sanctum where only the self exists.

Once within, consider those "dark" aspects of self and accept them for what they are; an opportunity to grow! Also consider the beauty of the darkness, the balance it gives to daylight; the chance it presents to rest and be refreshed.

Stay in your cocoon as long as you like. Accept its warmth and comforting. Accept any changes it offers at this junction. When you are ready, unravel the cocoon in the same manner it was built, returning the strands to your chakras. Make notes of your experience.

Shedding Old Skins (Exercise 2)

Part of the internal cocoon process is relinquishing the old. Throughout life we face situations that change who we are, how we react, and how we think. Sometimes tragic, sometimes happy, sometimes eye-opening, these circumstances write heavily on the chalk board of our lives, leaving marks that can not be erased. From marriage, to automobile accidents, to the birth of a child, or the death of a loved one, when the emotional dust settles we find ourselves slightly different than before.

Such experiences can not help but change us. Suddenly we discover the old shoes don't quite fit any more, but we have no idea how to remove them! This exercise is meant to help with that process.

Return to your cocoon. This time, however, before starting the visualization choose one or two items that represent the "old ways" of thinking. For example, if you are tired of polluting your body with cigarettes, these can become the symbol you keep with you during this exercise.₃ No matter what icon you choose, make sure it has deep personal significance in relation to your situation, and is something you don't mind being without afterwards.

Next, weave your cocoon as before, leaving a small hole near one foot at the bottom. Do not focus all your attention on that opening, just be aware that it exists. Take a few moments to settle back into your gestative mind-set, rehashing all the things that have happened recently. Try and take a step back from yourself and see your life as if it were a movie that you can critique or praise without remorse.

Now consider the "old way" you want to alter. Take the object you have chosen from its resting spot and hold it. Consider all the reasons why it is not a positive part of the sacred self. Pour all your negative feelings into that object. If it is safely crushable, break it in your hands then let it fall to the floor. Otherwise, stomp it with your foot thereby symbolically showing your intention to literally break away from that negativity.

Finally, kick it out of your cocoon through the opening you left earlier. Do not look to see where it goes. It is no longer part of you — it is not welcome in your metamorphic sanctuary. Just neatly close up the hole and rest within, allowing change to take its course.₄

With some habits and ideas this exercise may require several repetitions and a lot of personal effort to be effective. Life-long practices are rarely turned on and off like hot and cold running water. With time and patience, your cocoon can become a central classroom for the transformational journey towards Sacred Beauty.

Growing Wings
"Lend me the stone strength of the past, and I will lend you the wings of the future."
— Robinson Jeffers

With at least part of the past firmly behind us, and honest attempts toward rediscovering wholeness, the first signs of wings begin to form. We start thinking about ourselves and our world differently, with more positive and assured demeanors. We stop feeling like a victim of circumstance and become active participants towards creating a successful future. Most importantly we start speaking up when we, or those we care about, have been wronged.

There may be some hesitancy at this stage. We're not completely sure about how or when to employ these new personality traits. Sometimes this new persona feels as awkward as a baby with a full diaper. Basically, your wings are not dry yet, nor strong enough for much more than brief jaunts into the exciting realms of self sufficiency and independence.

You may find you make some errors in judgement at this point, like going a little over board, or not being persuasive enough. These are normal, and a perfectly acceptable part of learning to employ completely new skills. Like any good crafts person, you are trying each tool, each facet of the sacred self as it applies in a variety of situations.

As tempting as it is to slip back into old critical patterns, try not to berate yourself for small mishaps. Simply chalk it up to experience, make whatever amends are necessary and move on with tenacity in your back pocket. This is a period when you will learn the best times for words, and silence, action and retreat. You will master the ability of how to gracefully say "no" when other needs are more pressing, or happily say "yes."

Someone said that good things come in small packages. Life itself is now your package, one that is slowly opening all its treasures, just as you are opening your wings. Mind you, it may not always arrive with the exact bows, bells, squeaks and gongs you expected, but make the most of it. Take this opportunity to let your wings grow to their full strength and beauty, accepting all the lessons that go with this process.

Breaking The Cocoon

"His imagination resembled the wings of an ostrich. It enabled him to run, though not to soar."

— Lord Macaulay

There are many cocoons in our lives from which to break free. The first cocoon is the womb itself, next is walking freely, talking, and eventually removing ourselves from that safe, sheltered environment to become adults. Even in adult life, the cocoons continue to sprout around us; a job that is long outgrown, an unhealthy relationship, habits that ensnare us.

We have the capacity, the desire and the mental fortitude for change, meaning we can break free of our cocoons whenever we recognize the first signs that our wings are ready. Perhaps you suddenly discover a yearning to return to school, learn or refine a craft, go out dancing with an old friend for the first time in years, or just experience life more fully in some way. All of these things are pretty definite signs that a change has occurred within, and wants to manifest in action, without.

Not all of life's whims are practical, possible or even safe. For the obtainable ones, however, what holds us back from walking out on that limb? Are there old nagging doubts, harsh words from peers, or even perhaps the chastisement of your parents still lingering in the back of your mind? Breaking the cocoon means being willing to release those constraints once and for all. Otherwise, no matter how beautiful or big your wings become, there will be strings that tie you forever to the ground.

Hammer it Out (Exercise 3)

As before, return to your cocoon. Settle into what is now a familiar place of peaceful thought. Take time to assimilate the changes that have been happening so rapidly in your life. Examine your dreams, your desires, your goals. Know that just outside that cocoon your full potential awaits you. It is there, but first you must tear down the wall.

In your mind's eye, take a hammer or scissors and move it soundly into the weave. Hear the shell resonate with your desire to be free; your desire to emerge to a new beginning. Each time you hit the tapestry say, "I will be free, I will fly!"

Continue until the fabric of your cocoon gives way, shattering outward in hundreds of little fragments that can not be reassembled. As it bursts, a tremendous light greets you and a feeling of floating, of being totally liberated from burdens, doubts and troubles. Take a look at the surroundings just beyond the now shattered cocoon. They are lush, vibrant and as full of life as are you. This is your new terrain in which to grow and learn . . . a new frontier for the butterfly of your soul to explore.

Make sure to note everything you saw and heard during this exercise in your journal. Many times the information will be prophetic, insightful and helpful in the days ahead.

The Butterfly

"I'd be a butterfly born in a bower, where roses and lilies and violets meet"

— Thomas H. Bayly

Despite the beauty, grace and seeming ease of flight that so becomes the butterfly, it is not without enemies or troubles of its own. Having wings grants alternative outlooks, improved movement, a kind of refinement and poise, but it is not the absolute answer to all of life's snags. Even the spirit on wing must recognize that there are some limits, some horizons for which we may not be ready, some niches in life that we were never meant to fulfill.

This understanding does not keep the butterfly from being any less lovely, or any less a master of the winds. It is simply an awareness, carried skillfully balance with other realities; a deep knowingness that your movement through the universe is just as it should be.

Taking to Flight (Exercise 4)

Everything else is in place, but one last step remains; that of flying itself. Somehow, nature is kind in that the butterfly just seems to know how to dance on every breeze, and move with calm assurance in its new environment. People are not quite so fortunate. Even at this point we find ourselves a little leery, a little hesitant to step away from that complacent mold and become our life's keeper. Once this step is taken, your life will never be the same.

You need no longer return to the cocoon for this visualization. That part of your life is broken completely away. Instead, for this visualization begin back in the lovely glade, the first place you envisioned after being freed from the dark sanctuary. Smell the energy in the air, feel the winds as they move across your skin. See yourself with wings extending down from your hands to your hips, taking whatever shape is comfortable.

Make note of the type of wings you see. Are you a butterfly, or perhaps a kind of bird? You can look up any associations for that creature after the meditation and see if there's a symbolic message. Now stretch out those wings. Feel how strong and secure they are; how much a part of you they have become.

These are your spirit-wings that can take you many places, and most importantly grant new perspectives. When you are too close to a situation, soar to a better elevation and glimpse the bigger picture. Or, when you feel the need to let loose, come to this place and frolic with the winds. Let your spirit be refreshed.

The gift of the butterfly is one that extends no "quick fixes." It is a slow legacy, played out on the stage of your life each day. It is one that allows you to rise above circumstance to find some measure of success, joy, hope, and learning in every situation you encounter. In the end, the greatest treasure the butterfly offers us is wings of peace; peace with self, peace with others, and peace with our planet. Fly gently to your destiny.

Atop The Flower of The World

"The whole difference between construction and creation is exactly this; that a thing constructed can only be loved after it is constructed; but a thing created is loved before it exists."

— Gilber K. Chesterton

Here ends and begins your journey. As you walk the path of Beauty, each day and each moment is both final and just starting. Like a giant circle of sparkling creation, your feet now meet the earth with new vitality. Each lesson learned leads to new questions, new insight and new adventures.

What now, you ask? Once your quest for wholeness seems fulfilled, then what? Then your task becomes one of a guide, of reaching out and helping others who find the way too long or too hard. Give them the benefit of your wisdom and experiences so their Path can be less difficult than the one you followed.

In truth you will find the quest for the Sacred Self never really ends. Today and tomorrow, your soul will always desire to be closer to the Divine source. The world is forever your flower to explore, and you have the wings of spirit to guide you. Capture that inquiring zest, that curiosity that makes every moment in life a miracle; a wonder to behold. Fly unfettered above your blossom, and know that you have had some part in creating that loveliness. And, finally, always remember to land periodically, so that your sacred self has one foot on the ground, but dreams and hopes that soar with the eagles.

You are the Beauty. You are the Magic. You are the Sacredness. Know it, feel it, live it!

Be Blessed.

Notes

5. The Devic kingdom is elemental in nature, but most often closely aligned with a particular plant, flower or other natural object. Sometimes fairies are considered a kind of Deva.

2. A charm is generally defined as any object that is influenced by, or protected by, magic. Frequently charms are empowered by spells, incantations and various herbal substances in order to produce a specific effect on the bearer.

3. Any number of items can be found at places that carry dollhouse supplies.

4. When you have completed this visualization, it is suggested that you burn, throw away or bury that symbol later so that it is literally "dead" to you.

Personal Afterword

"Perseverance is more prevailing than violence; and many things which can not be overcome when they are together, yield themselves up when taken little by little"

— Plutarch

Every day we hear about violent crimes: rape, mental subjugation, beatings and overt cruelty, not only towards the sexes but also creeds and colors. It is difficult to know exactly what has lead to this upsurge in peoples' inhumanity towards each other. At least one part of the picture is an overwhelmed judicial system who often must accept expediency over true equity. Another part of the problem is the overwhelming numbers of people who have carefully sequestered their spiritual self from the rest of reality, leaving decency and the conscious behind as well. Then too, there is the terrible apathy bug that shrugs its shoulders and says, "that's life," or worse yet, ignores the problem in favor of a prettier picture.

No matter the reasons for violence in our society, those of us walking the Path of Beauty can not continue to let it flow by us with as much disregard as an automobile on the street. Ours is a trust to try and bring about change not only within ourselves but our world, and this particular point is certainly one of great need. If we have been fortunate not to have been touched by violence, our charge is one of helping those who have to reclaim their sanctity. Our duty is also one to assist people wrongly accused of atrocities by those with greed, intolerance or revenge on their hearts.

People who have been traumatized by mental or physical violence experience devastation to the body-mind-and soul balance. Violence tears at the very fibers of personal sanctity and steals our sense of control. For these individuals, their first responsibility is to their own heart; to find a way to begin the healing. Very often this means reaching out for help; be it family, friends or clergy. While often the most difficult step to make when guilt, confusion and fear ravage your mind, it is also the best step. There is nothing shameful about needing an non-judgmental ear and some sound advise.

Sometimes legal action is also called for, but do not be pressured by anyone into this step. The word "prosecute" is bantered about easily by those who are not suffering. Unfortunately, the court system can be twice as demeaning as the situation itself. If you are ready for such a battle, know that you have the chance to stop the brutality at least for a while, and maybe preserve someone else from anguish. This is a decision you alone can make.

My prayer is that someday our world will come to know its Divine nature in an intimate enough manner that such crimes will all but disappear. In the mean time, I must trust the immutable human spirit and the love of true spiritual seekers to us to heal these wounds. This also means putting aside matters of personal opinion for the greater good — the longevity and well-being of our entire race. Let us guard harmony with each other as dearly as we hold it in our own hearts. Peace.

Appendix
Goods and Services

The following list of groups, organizations and businesses is provided in an effort to pass on positive, life affirming goods and services to readers within the range of my research and knowledge. They are listed in alphabetical order with a brief description and cost of catalogue (if applicable). **In all cases, it is best to enclose a SASE with any request for information.**

* **American Association of Sex Educators, Counselors & Therapists**
  435 N. Michigan Ave. Suite 1717
  Chicago IL 60611
  (312) 644-0828

Perhaps one of the best resources to help you find options for sex therapy in your region.

* **American Dance Therapy Association**
  2000 Country Plaza, Suite 108
  Columbia MD 21044
  (410) 997-4040

Information on the use of dance to improve personal well-being. They should be able to provide you with a list of any teachers or classes which are on-going in your area.

* **Arawn Machia**
  5300 NE 24, Ter 224
  Ft. Lauderdale, FL 33308

Internationally recognized spiritual councilor, psychologist, Reiki Master, lecturer and High Priest of Strega (Italian Wicca). Has tons of valuable information and knowledge regarding diverse forms of healing.

- **Association for Research & Enlightenment**
  Box 595, 67th Street & Atlantic Avenue
  Virginia Beach, VA 23451

This group was founded by Edgar Cayce, a great psychic and humanitarian, nearly 100 years ago. They have a lending library for members along with hundreds of tapes and books on spiritual self improvement.

- **Boston Alliance for Gay and Lesbian Youth**
  Box 814
  Boston MA 02103 (800) 42BAGLY

A unique organization which works with the younger sector of individuals who discover their sexual leanings early in life.

- **Chicago Women's Health Center**
  3435 North Sheffield
  Chicago, IL 60657
  (312) 935-6126

A terrific central resource for women seeking alternative methods of impregnation with or without a partner.

- **Circle Network News**
  Box 219
  Mt. Horeb, WI 53572

An organization which has seen more than its fair share of legal battles over freedom of religion. Quarterly newsletter includes articles on positive approaches for alternative faiths and updates on legal issues pertaining to religious freedom. Write for subscription information.

- **Co-Op America**
  Box 14140
  Madison WI 53704
  (608)-256-5522

An organization which has lots of practical information on environmental issues and a catalogue of earth-safe products including those for house care and pets. SASE for catalogue.

- **CraftWise**
  Box 457
  Botsford CT 06404
  203-374-6475

A wonderful group dedicated to bringing the diversity of New Age ideals to people around the US through four annual gatherings in different regions. Schedules of events, locations, and speakers available. Write to be placed on their mailing list.

- **Daughters of Isis**
  577 Sample Rd.
  Pompano Beach FL 33064
  305-941-4081

An incredible little gift shop filled with some of the most unique New Age items I've seen. Terrific service, weekly tea/coffee house. Other events.

- **Direct Marketing Association**
  6 East 43rd Street
  New York, NY 10017

If you're tired of bulk mail which only ends up in your recycling bin, write to these people and request having your name and address removed from their lists.

- **Earth Dance Music**
  Box 5565
  Sherman Oaks CA 91413

Wonderful instrumentals that blend the best of history with modern vision.

- **Emerge**
  18 Hurley St.
  Cambridge, MA 02141

A pioneer group working specifically with men who have strong tendencies toward physical violence.

- **Enchanted Apothecary**
  72-01 Austin St.
  Forest Hills NY 11325
  718-261-5006

New Age/Magical gift items, artwork, native dream catchers, and regular lectures. Catalogue available.

- **Environmental Defense Fund**
  444 Park Avenue South
  New York, NY 10016

Stay up to date and informed on litigation pertaining to important environmental issues. Newsletter available.

- **Frontier Herbs**
  Box 299
  Norway IA 52318
  1-800-669-3275

Organic herbs, cut and sifted, accessories and some gift items.

Excellent shipping times and very reasonable prices.

- **Geneva's Greetings**
  Box 3132 CRS
  Johnson City TN 37602

Thematic New Age greeting cards, book marks, booklets on various subjects, forthcoming calenders and other gift items.

- **Global Pacific Music**
  1275 E. MacArthur
  Sonoma CA 95476
  707-996-2748

Music dedicated to the Village of Earth. Terrific selection!

- **Good Vibrations**
  126 Valencia St.
  San Francisco CA   94110
  (415) 550-7399

A store with everything from books to "toys" to help improve sexual enjoyment, understanding and gratification for both partners. Bits of sound advise are given in their catalogue.

- **Granny's Old Fashioned Products**
  3581 E. Milton
  Pasadena CA 91107

A company which offers environmentally safe cleaning products for the home along with many other items.

- **Gray Panthers**
  1424 Sixteenth Street NW, Suite 602
  Washington DC 20036
  (202) 387-3111

A marvelous organization who focuses on the social problems, potentials and needs among the elderly. Newsletter available.

- **Homeopathic Educational Services**
  2124 Kittredge St.
  Berkeley, CA 94704
  (800) 359-9051

Important to our computerized society, this organization even has software on homeopathics alongside books and study tapes.

- **Hourglass Creations & Maille Order**
  492 Breckenridge
  Buffalo, NY 14213

A mail-order, earth-aware business with a unique line of home made soaps, massage and perfume oils, body powders, skin creams, lineament, incense, some bulk herbs, etc. Also custom sewing, leather work and chain maille products available. SASE for catalogue.

- **Koziara, Colleen**
  405 S. Wheaton
  Wheaton IL 60187

Illustrator/artist for small or large pieces, various background and mediums.

- **Kym's Creations**
  Box 178
  Pentwater MI 49449

Kym makes marvelous Pagan style rosaries fashioned after the older tradition to honor the Goddess aspect. She also is a tremendous resource for individuals seeking midwives and good advise on pregnancy. Please send SASE for details.

- **Lotus Light**
  Box 2
  Milmot WI 53192

A wonderful operation which carries everything from cruelty free makeups, soaps and skin care products to organic bulk herbs and bachs flower essences. Very timely service and delivery.

- **MAGIC**
  1924 Wood Unit A
  Texarcana TX 75503

An cooperative of artists committed to helping promote each other's talents, and whose efforts are aimed at creating a vision for the earth that is whole and united. MAGICal artists believe that everyone has a special gift to share. Quarterly newsletter $10.00; Artist membership $15.00; Professional members $20.00.

- **National Center for Homeopathy**
  801 N. Fairfax St., Suite 306
  Alexandria VA 22314
  (703) 548-7790

This organization has a monthly newsletter, several nationally extended groups, books and basic information on Homeopathics.

- **National Gay and Lesbian Task Force**
  1734 14th Street NW
  Washington DC 20009
  (202) 332-6483

An extensive listing of referrals and publications that help those struggling with sexuality or those trying to understand friends/family members who have come "out of the closet".

- **Pagan Educational Network**
  Box 1364
  Bloomington IN 47402-1364

A pagan networking group with the motto "do what you can, when you can". They are a non-profit organization dedicated to public education about Paganism as well as trying to help build and strengthen the internal pagan community. Civil rights and freedom of worship information available. Associate membership $12.00 includes annual newsletter.

- **Phoenix & Dragon**
  300 Hammond Dr.
  Atlanta, GA 30328

Incredible jewelry; this store is stuffed full in every corner with wonderful books, gifts, music, and more!

- **Rocky Mountain Enterprises**
  364 W. 13th Ave.
  Homestead PA 15120
  800-829-0198

Have you always wanted simple, beautiful, and hand crafted musical instruments to bring the sounds of resplendence into your home? This is the place to go. RME offers *numbered* music so almost anyone can play a tune, write their own inspired music, etc. They also have interest free payment plans and lifetime guarantees on all their goods. Call for a catalogue.

- **Rodale Press**
  33 E. Minor St.
  Emmaus PA 18049

Current publications, fairly priced on self help, especially organic foods, gardening and nutrition. Very good order times.

- **Shell & Stone Productions**
  c/o Feavearyear
  176 Virginia St.
  Rochester, NY 14619

A variety of custom made useful items and decorations for the home in wood or stained glass. Please send a full description of the type of item you desire for quote with SASE.

- **Silver Challice**
  RR 1, Box 680
  Central Ave.
  Westville NJ 08093

A journal dedicated to magical/New Age topics in open forum. Special features include legal focus, humor and regular writers.

- **Spellbound Books**
  480 Washington Ave.
  Belleville NJ 07109

- **Spellbound West**
  11116 Magnolia Blvd.
  W. Hollywood CA 91602

Candles, dream catchers, books, jewelry and wonderful gifts for the New Age.

- **Swift, Jackie**
  10084 Hooker Hill Rd.
  Perrysburg, NY 14129

A full line of home grown herbs and herbal products with a truly loving touch added for good measure! SASE for price list.

- **United Federation of Pagans**
  Box 6006
  Athens, Ga 30604

A group whose motto, "Unity through Diversity" says it all. Generally speaking, this organization has mostly other groups as members. Individual may write, however, to try and find people in their area to work with.

- **Washington Rape Crisis Center**
  Box 21005
  Washington DC 20009

The DC Rape Crisis Center rendered a significant contribution in starting many related projects and educating the public on the Rape reality. Their publication on starting such a center is $5.00 and is excellent.

- **Wish Fulfilling Tree**
  Betty McKeon
  2329B Cheshire bridge Rd.
  Atlanta GA 30324

Gift shop with tons of books and terrific folks to help you find anything you need.

Bibliography

Adair, Margo; *Working Inside Out*, Wingbow Press, Berkley CA 1984.

Andrews, Ted; *Sacred Sounds*, Llewellyn Publications, St. Paul, MN 1993.

Baker, Margaret; *Folklore and Customs of Rural England*, Rowman & Littlefield, Totawa NJ 1974.

Bartlett, John; *Familiar Quotations*, Little Brown & Company, Boston MA, 1938.

Bates, Marilyn & Keirsey, David; *Please Understand Me*, Prometheus Nemesis Books, California, 1978.

Berger, John; *Ways of Seeing*, Penguin Press, London England, 1988

Beyerl, Paul; *Master Book of Herbalism*, Phoenix Publishing, Custer WA 1984.

Black, William G.; *Folk Medicine*, Burt Franklin Co., New York, NY 1883.

Blumenfeld, Warren J; *Looking at Gay and Lesbian Life*, Beacon Press, Boston MA 1988.

Bolen, Jean Shinoda, MD; *The Goddess in Every Woman*, Harper Colophon Publishing, New York, NY 1985.

Borysenko, Joan; *Minding Our Bodies, Mending the Mind*, Addison-Wesley, Reading MA 1987.

Brody, Jane; *Jane Brody's Nutrition Book*, Bantam Books, NY 1987

Budge, EA Wallis; *Amulets & Talismans*, University Books, New Hyde Park, NY 1968.

Chase, A.W., MD; *Receipt Book & Household Physician*, F.B. Dickerson Company, Detroit, MI 1908.

Clarkson, Rosetta, *Green Enchantment*, McMillian Publishing, New York, NY 1940.

Cooley, Arnold J.; *The Toilet in Ancient & Modern Times*, J.B. Lippincott & Company, Philadelphia PA, 1873.

Cross, Jean; *In Grandmother's Day*, Prentice Hall, Englewood Cliffs NJ 1980.

Culpeper, Nicholas; *The Complete Herbal*, W. Foulsham, London England, 1952.

Cunningham, Scott; *Encyclopedia of Magical Herbs*, Llewellyn Publications, St. Paul, MN 1988.

_____; *The Magic in Food*, Llewellyn Publications, ST. Paul, MN 1991.

_____; *The Magic of Incense*, Oils and Brews, Llewellyn Publications, St. Paul, MN 1988.

Davison, Michael Worth, Editor; *Everyday Life through the Ages*, Readers Digest Association, London England, 1992.

Drury, Nevill; *Dictionary of Mysticism & the Occult*, Harper and Row, New York, NY 1985.

Erikson, Erik; *Childhood & Society 2nd Edition*, Norton, New York, 1963.

Farrar, Janet & Stewart; *The Witches' God*, Phoenix Publishing, Custer WA, 1989.

_____; *The Witches Goddess*, Phoenix Publishing, Custer WA 19__.

Fielding, William J.; *Strange Superstitions & Magical Practices*, Paperback Library, New York NY 1968.

Finley, Guy; *The Secret of Letting Go*, Llewellyn Publications, St. Paul MN 1992.

_____; *The Secret Way of Wonder*, Llewellyn Publications, St. Paul MN 1993.

Firestone, Shulamith; *The Dialect of Sex*, Bantam Books, New York, 1971.

Fitch, Ed; *The Rites of Odin*, Llewellyn Publications, St. Paul, MN 1990.

Fox, William MD; *Model Botanic Guide to Health*, Sheffield Press, Fargate, 1907.

Freud, S; *Introductory Lectures to Psychoanalysis*, Boni & Liveright, NY 1920.

Fromm, E.; *Escape from Freedom*, Farrar & Reinhart, NY 1941.

Haggard, Howard, MD; *Mystery, Magic & Medicine*, Double Day and Co., Garden City NJ, 1933.

Hall, Manly; *Secret Teachings of All Ages*, Philosophical Research Society, Los Angeles CA 1977.

Hechtlinger, Adelaide; *The Seasonal Hearth*, Overlook Press, New York, NY 1986.

Hutchinson, Ruth & Adams, Ruth; *Every Day's a Holiday*, Harper & Brothers, New York, NY 1951.

Jung. C; *Psychological Types*, Harcourt Brace, NY 1923.

Kieckhefer, Richard; *Magic in the Middle Ages*, Cambridge University Press, Melbourne Australia, 1989.

Kreiger, Dolores; *The Therapeutic Touch*, Prentice Hall, Englewood Cliffs, NJ 1979.

Leach, Maria, editor; *Standard Dictionary of Folklore*, Mythology and Legend, Funk & Wagnall, NY 1972.

Lorie, Peter; *Superstitions*, Simon & Schuster, New York NY 1992.

Magnall, Richmal; *Historical and Miscellaneous Questions*, Longman, Brown, Green and Longman, London England, 1850.

Maslow, A.; *Motivation & Personality*, Harper, NY 1954.

Metzner, Ralph; *Know Your Type*, Doubleday, New York, 1979.

Millett, Kate; *Sexual Politics*, Virago Press, London England, 1985.

Murray, Keith; *Ancient Rites & Ceremonies*, Tudor Press, Toronto Canada, 1980.

Opie, Iona & Tatem, Moria; *Dictionary of Superstitions*, Oxford University Press, New York NY 1989.

Our Bodies, Ourselves (new edition); Touchstone Books, NY 1992.

Read, Sir Herbert, editor; *Collected Works of C.G. Jung*, Princeton University Press, NJ, 1966.

Reed, Evelyn; *Sexism & Science*, Pathfinder Press, NY 1978.

Scarf, Maggie; *Intimate Partners*, Ballentine Books, NY 1987.

Scott, Rev. Loughran; *Bullfinch's Age of Fable*, David McKay Publishing, Washington Square PA 1898.

Sheehy, Gail; *Passages*, Dutton, New York, 1977.

Singer, Charles; *From Magic to Science*, Dover Books, NY 1958.

Slagle, Kate W.; *Live with Loss*, Prentice Hall, Englewood Cliffs NJ 1982.

Stevens, Anthony; *Archetypes: A New History of the Self*, Morrow, New York, 1982.

Telesco, Patricia; *Folkways*, Llewellyn Publications, St. Paul, MN 1994.

_____; *A Victorian Grimoire*, Llewellyn Publications, St. Paul MN 1992.

Tuleja Tad; *Curious Customs*, Harmony Books, New York 1987.

Walker, Barbara; *Womens Dictionary of Symbols & Sacred Objects*, Harper Row Publishing, SanFrancisco Ca 1988.

Websters Universal Unabridged Dictionary; World Syndicate Publishing, New York NY 1937.

Williams Jude; *Jude's Herbal*, Llewellyn Publications, St. Paul, MN 1992.

Wolf, Naomi; *The Beauty Myth*, William Morrow & Company, New York, 1991.

Wootton A.; *Animal Folklore*, Myth & Legend, Blanford Press, New York 1986.

More from Blue Star Productions

Mirror, Mirror: Reflections of the Sacred Self, Telesco	10.95
Rhiannon, Dodd	10.95
The Emerald of Lastanzia, Dodd	12.95
Me 'n God in the Coffee Shop, Donovan	10.95
The Antilles Incident, Todd	6.95
From the Hearts of Angels, Dezra	12.95
Little Book of Angels, Dezra	6.95
Little Book of Angels Reflections Journal, Dezra	5.95
The Best Kept Secrets, Wright	12.95
365 Days of Prosperity, Telesco	5.95
365 Days of Luck, Telesco	5.95
365 Days of Health, Telesco	5.95
Cataclysms?? A New Look at Earth Changes, Hickox	12.95
The Knowing, Bates	15.95
A Question of Time, Bryce	6.95
The Ascent: Doorway to Eternity, Cross	8.95
Dance on the Water, Leffers	12.95

Check your local bookstore or use the order form below

Credit card orders (MC/Visa): Call 1-888-262-7090. Or, send check or money order, plus $5 s/h for one book, $1.00 for each additional book to: Book World, Inc, 9666 E Riggs Rd #194, Sun Lakes AZ 85248.

Name: _____

Address: _____

City: _____ State: _____ Zip:_____

Visa/MC No. _____Exp. Date:_____

Signature: _____

Prices reflect U.S. only; foreign orders: add $7.00 per book.
Please allow 4-6 weeks for delivery

More from Book World, Inc.

Mission to Sonora, Cramer	10.95
Trail of Darkness, Jensen	14.95
Saintly Death, Sainsbury	10.95
Flight of the Hawk: The Aaron Pryor Story, Pryor	14.95
Brothers of the Pine, Simmons	15.95
Apache Tears, Mustain & Livingston	15.95
How to Write A Bestseller in 40 Days or Less, DeBolt	9.95
An Author's Guide to Budget Book Promotion, Leffers	5.95

Check your local bookstore or use the order form below

Credit card orders (MC/Visa): Call 1-888-262-7090. Or, send check or money order, plus $5 s/h for one book, $1.00 for each additional book to: Book World, Inc, 9666 E Riggs Rd #194, Sun Lakes AZ 85248.

Name: _____

Address: _____

City: _____ State: _____ Zip: _____

Visa/MC No. _____ Exp. Date: _____

Signature: _____

Prices reflect U.S. only; foreign orders: add $7.00 per book.
Please allow 4-6 weeks for delivery